Jacqueline Schmittem

Data-driven travel marketing

Internet Economics
Internetökonomie

edited by
herausgegeben von

Prof. Dr. Julia Maintz
(Cologne Business School (CBS) –
European University of Applied Sciences)

Volume / Band 11

LIT

Jacqueline Schmittem

Data-driven travel marketing
The importance of business intelligence for affiliate marketing in the travel industry

LIT

Cover image: © Jacqueline Schmittem

This book is printed on acid-free paper.

Bibliographic information published by the Deutsche Nationalbibliothek
The Deutsche Nationalbibliothek lists this publication in the Deutsche Nationalbibliografie; detailed bibliographic data are available in the Internet at http://dnb.dnb.de.

ISBN 978-3-643-91334-0 (pb)
ISBN 978-3-643-96334-5 (PDF)

A catalogue record for this book is available from the British Library.

© LIT VERLAG GmbH & Co. KG Wien,
Zweigniederlassung Zürich 2021
Flössergasse 10
CH-8001 Zürich
Tel. +41 (0) 76-632 84 35
E-Mail: zuerich@lit-verlag.ch   https://www.lit-verlag.ch
Distribution:
In the UK: Global Book Marketing, e-mail: mo@centralbooks.com
In North America: Independent Publishers Group, e-mail: orders@ipgbook.com
In Germany: LIT Verlag Fresnostr. 2, D-48159 Münster
Tel. +49 (0) 2 51-620 32 22, Fax +49 (0) 2 51-922 60 99, e-mail: vertrieb@lit-verlag.de

PREFACE

The global economy is more than ever driven by insights gained from the analysis of big data. In this hyper-competitive global environment, it is of pivotal importance for companies to realize a strategic positioning based on the interdisciplinary usage of insights from corporate data. Business intelligence tools allow to harvest and analyse available data of any kind in real-time. They consequently serve as key resources for the continuous monitoring and adjustment of a company's strategic alignment.

In this paper, Jacqueline Schmittem explores cutting-edge approaches in the rapidly evolving landscape of business intelligence tools and techniques. She provides an in-depth analysis of the potential of business intelligence in the context of affiliate marketing in the travel industry. Her study is a must-read for marketers in the travel industry. Moreover, her findings are of high relevance for corporate experts seeking to apply business intelligence tools and techniques in any discipline and industry.

Julia Maintz

Professor of Internet Economics and International Management, CBS International Business School

Table of content

1	Introduction	5
1.1	Purpose	7
1.2	Structure	7
2	Business intelligence	9
2.1	Definition and differentiation	9
2.2	Components of the business intelligence process	11
2.2.1	Big data	11
2.2.2	Business intelligence tools	13
2.2.3	Data-driven and needs-driven decision-making	14
2.3	Business intelligence agility, maturity, and acceptance	16
2.3.1	Business intelligence agility	16
2.3.2	Business intelligence maturity	17
2.3.3	Business intelligence acceptance	19
2.4	Opportunities for companies	20
2.5	Challenges for companies	22
3	Affiliate marketing	25
3.1	Definition and differentiation	25
3.2	Fundamentals of affiliate marketing	26
3.2.1	Functional principle	27
3.2.2	External affiliate network vs. in-house affiliate network	29
3.2.3	Commission models	32
3.2.4	Tracking methods and affiliate fraud	33
3.3	Importance of affiliate marketing	36
3.3.1	Opportunities for companies	36

Table of content

3.3.2 Affiliate marketing in the overall online marketing mix 38
3.4 Affiliate marketing and the travel industry 39
3.4.1 Differentiation of online travel marketing actors 40
3.4.2 The value of affiliate marketing for the travel industry 41
4 Methodology 45
4.1 Research method 45
4.2 Sample selection 46
4.3 Data analysis technique 47
5 The importance of business intelligence in affiliate marketing . 49
5.1 Targeting and retargeting 49
5.2 General marketing decision process 52
5.3 Efficiency and must-dos of business intelligence integration ... 55
5.4 Limitation of business intelligence application 58
5.5 Interim conclusion 60
5.6 Travel marketing 60
5.6.1 General value of affiliate marketing for the travel industry 61
5.6.2 Business intelligence in affiliate travel marketing 64
6 Conclusion 69
7 Recommendations 73
7.1 Practical recommendations 73
7.2 Recommendations for future research 74
8 Limitations of study 75
9 Reference list 77
Appendix I

	Table of figures	
Figure 1	The simplified principle of business intelligence	11
Figure 2	Business intelligence and performance management maturity model	19
Figure 3	Illustration of the affiliate marketing principle	29

1 INTRODUCTION

In the digital era, companies are starting to become interested into expanding their business activities to the digital world. E-commerce offers companies the opportunity to display their products and services in an environment that is specialised in cutting costs and time for searching for the best products at the best prices available (Purnamasari et al., 2019, p. 1). Having said this, the rise of e-commerce offers companies the opportunity to operate on a global market and enter new markets, while simultaneously gaining access to new, potential customer segments. Furthermore, a large flexibility and up-to-dateness regarding the products and services offered can be guaranteed. This may lead to an increase of the competitiveness of a company. A main advantage of e-commerce is that companies are able to collect specific customer data by tracking the buying and search behaviour of customers on their website (Olbrich, Schultz, & Holsing, 2019, p. 22). It is a matter of fact, that due to the ever-evolving globalisation, teamwork and sharing data is becoming a huge topic for companies nowadays. In order to drive the success of a company, it is inevitable for businesses to be creative and agile in their way of operating. Here, the concept of business intelligence comes into play (Brito, Briegas, & Iglesias, 2019, p. 156). Business intelligence can be seen as a holistic and company-wide approach that helps businesses to extract valuable information out of different data sets being harvested (Kemper, Baars, & Mehanna, 2010, p. 8). Furthermore, business intelligence has to be considered as an umbrella term for collecting, storing, processing, and analysing different data sets with the aim of gaining valuable insights. These insights are then used for increasing the efficiency and competitiveness of a company (Larson & Chang, 2016, p. 701). In addition, the integration of business intelligence technologies can help businesses to create further customer value along the value chain (Ram, Zhang, & Koronios, 2016, p. 223) by establishing a data-driven decision-making process among all managers and employees. Consequently, an increase of the effectiveness and further efficiency of the decision-making process is assured (Rhyn & Blohm, 2019, p. 4).

Another important topic, being highly relevant nowadays, is the approach of affiliate marketing. In the digital era, companies have to constantly rethink their business models and marketers have to rethink their way of communicating to the existing and potential customer base (Morozan & Enache, 2013, p. 880). As a consequence, a lot of different online marketing channels have emerged, helping companies to market their products to a variety of people and without any time limitations (Pathak & Saxena, 2019, p. 352). One of these approaches is affiliate marketing, a performance-based digital marketing channel that is offering companies the opportunity to market their products on an external website for a certain commission fee (Kasilingam & Thanuja, 2020, p. 4222). In addition, by helping companies with generating additional sales and building a certain brand awareness, affiliate marketing has proven to be one of the most important online marketing channels (Denzin, 2019, p. 4; Suchada et al., 2017, p. 132). Even though affiliate marketing is one of the oldest online marketing techniques (Bormann, 2019, p. 21), it is perceived as one of the most important channels, having "a significant effect on organization's product visibility, advertising cost, and return on investment (ROI)" (Patrick & Hee, 2019, p. 702). Having said this, the travel industry has proven to be particularly capable of adapting to newly evolving requirements of the digitalisation and the potential acquisition of international markets. Furthermore, the digitalisation has increased the overall competitiveness of travel companies by giving them the possibility to reach a large number of customers (Popescu, Nicolae, & Pavel, 2015, pp. 163–164). As a consequence, affiliate marketing has proven to be one of the most preferred marketing channels when talking about the travel industry. Having said this, it is perceived as an additional distribution channel, enhancing the overall sales figures and brand position of travel companies (Mariussen, Bowie, & Paraskevas, 2012, p. 1). In addition, it helps travel companies to formulate strategic alliances in order to develop complementary travel products and, as a consequence, helps the businesses to stay competitive in their respective markets (Middleton et al., 2009, p. 389; Wauyo, Omol, & Okumu, 2017, p. 60). Even though the topics of business intelligence and affiliate marketing are considered to be highly relevant these days, the research on the correlation of both of them with regard to the travel industry is non-existent.

1.1 PURPOSE

The purpose of this paper is to research and evaluate the importance of business intelligence for the online marketing channel affiliate marketing. Moreover, this importance is validated on the example of its application in travel marketing. Consequently, this leads to the two research questions being answered by the executed research: *To what extend does business intelligence help to make relevant affiliate marketing decisions?* (R1) and *Does business intelligence improve the efficiency of affiliate marketing activities in online travel marketing?* (R2). This paper focuses on the importance of different aspects of business intelligence for both topics, affiliate marketing and travel marketing, in order to examine the different possible application fields of business intelligence properly.

1.2 STRUCTURE

The research conveyed follows the subsequently described structure:

The study starts with two chapters defining, differentiating, and examining all relevant aspects regarding the two main topics business intelligence (*chapter 2 et seq.*) and affiliate marketing (*chapter 3 et seq.*). The knowledge conveyed about these topics and their related aspects is based on previous academic research. This ensures that both subjects are highlighted through a lot of different insights. Subsequent to the theoretical research part, the methodology chapter (*4 et seq.*) will be explaining the research method applied and highlight the sample selection and data analysis technique used to conduct the practical research. After this chapter, the findings of the author's research are presented and linked to the previously defined research questions R1 and R2 (*chapter 5 et seq.*). This is followed by the author's conclusion (*chapter 6*). Last but not least, recommendations for future research and practical recommendations for the industry are given (*chapter 7 et seq.*) and the limitations of the study (*chapter 8*) are shown.

2 BUSINESS INTELLIGENCE

The purpose of this chapter is to give a broad overview of business intelligence. This refers to the definition and differentiation of the term, different components being involved in the business intelligence process, and the important topics of business intelligence agility, maturity, and acceptance. The chapter is going to be continued with the outlining of the opportunities and challenges coming along with business intelligence.

2.1 DEFINITION AND DIFFERENTIATION

During the last decades, a lot of different perceptions and definitions regarding the topic of business intelligence have emerged. However, these definition approaches either have their focus on the technical, information systems part or the functional and economical application in management policies (Schön, 2016, pp. 291–293). In the context of this research, the economical definition of business intelligence will be used in every respect. Hence, *business intelligence* can be defined as an IT-based and integrated approach to harvest, store, process, and analyse all data being available to a certain company. As a consequence, it has to be seen as an umbrella term for the technologies and processes being associated with these actions (Gaardboe & Svarre, 2018, p. 1). Furthermore, business intelligence is said to generate valuable and valid insights being visually prepared in order to distribute them throughout the whole organisation (Tableau, 2020). In this sense, the term *intelligence* is referring to the information that has to be processed in order to actually gain more company knowledge, so that costs can be reduced and the overall revenues of a company increase (Kemper, Baars, & Mehanna, 2010, p. 8). The framework of business intelligence is said to combine a company's resources, such as human capital, technology, data, and processes, in order to develop a knowledge-based strategy and constantly adapt to the dynamic business environment. By merging information from different sources, companies can benefit from business intelligence in various ways (being examined in *chapter 2.4*). Furthermore, the concept of business intelligence can be applied among a variety of different fields such as marketing, financial services, inventory control, or medical diagnosis (Alnoukari & Hanao, 2017, pp. 5–6). Having said this, business intelligence is always affected by its ever-changing environment. The business intelligence technologies have to constantly adapt to changing user needs, technical capabilities, and many more. This need for change can arise in many ways: from small to large and from short to long-term. It is crucial for companies to understand that business intelligence should not be seen as a one-time practice, but as an ongoing process being executed throughout the whole organisation (Yu, Lapouchnian, & Deng, 2013, p. 1). Last but not least, it is of high importance to differentiate business intelligence from other terms belonging to this field. These terms are the subsequent: big data, data warehouse(s), and big data analytics. In practice, those terms are often likely to be mixed up. It has to be considered, that the related terms are sub-actions of business intelligence and thus, shall not be used as synonyms for this holistic approach (Williams, 2016, pp. 28–29). In order to execute business intelligence successfully, big data is needed as the fundament of operating, being further examined in *chapter 2.2.1*. This fundament is subsequently stored and structured in, for example, a data warehouse. Data warehouses are repositories, being primarily concerned with the management of the data stacked. This data is often coming from a lot of different sources, being highly relevant for different business purposes (Holland, 2019, pp. 279–280; Pyae, 2018, p. 6). In order to properly process and analyse the data harvested, business intelligence tools such as big data analytics are needed. The general value of big data analytics is that it helps companies to process big data in real-time and helps to optimise business processes accordingly to the certain insights gained (Ram, Zang, & Koronios, 2016, p. 223). Having said this, more information about big data analytics is given in *chapter 2.2.2*. In order to simplify the principle and relationship of business intelligence and related terms, the subsequent figure has been developed:

Figure 1 **The simplified principle of business intelligence**

Sources 1–5 → Big data → Data warehouse → Business intelligence tools → Insights; Business intelligence tools also feed into Analysis and Visualization.

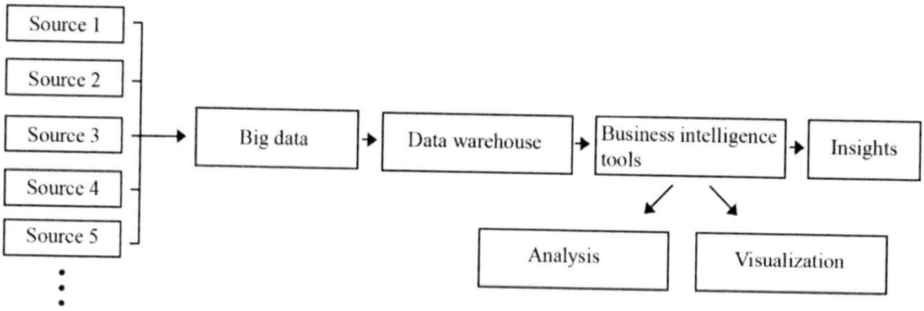

Note: own illustration

2.2 COMPONENTS OF THE BUSINESS INTELLIGENCE PROCESS

This chapter deals with the overall business intelligence process and different components being involved. Hereby, big data, business intelligence tools, and the decision-making process are outlined.

2.2.1 BIG DATA

Big data can be characterised as the core element of every business intelligence activity (Balakrishnan & Rahul, 2018, p. 21). It is the practical term for "a massive amount of data that can be analysed and used to make decisions" (Rafferty, Rafferty, & Hung, 2016, p. 1). In addition, big data has an immense capability of stimulating productivity, innovation, and the overall economy (Rafferty, Rafferty, & Hung, 2016, p. 3). Moreover, these enormous data sets have proven to exceed the ability of traditional data bases and data processing technologies (Oliveira et al., 2019, p. 691). The concept of big data combines data from different sources, such as social media, browsing history, geolocation, or purchasing behaviour. With the ongoing evolution of the digitalisation, the amount of different data sources and formats is perceived to increase constantly (Rafferty, Rafferty,

& Hung, 2016, pp. 2–3). Having said this, big data can be defined with the basic 3V concept: volume, variety, and velocity (Balakrishnan & Rahul, 2018, p. 21). In this context, volume describes the large amount of data being associated with the term big data. It is said that this amount is often perceived as the main challenge that businesses have to face, as it is simply too big to be handled by traditional algorithms or data storage systems (Zhou et al., 2014, p. 62). Variety, on the other hand, describes the characteristic that big data consists of data sets being generated by various, different sources. This always comes with the unavoidable aspect of data appearing in different formats and having to deal with structured and unstructured data sets (Huang et al., 2017, p. 1229). Structured data is seen as every data that can be easily described and visualised within a certain matrix, e.g. in columns and rows, whereas unstructured data is defined as data being hard to generalise, e.g. images, social media, and click streams (Kumar, 2017, pp. 32–33). The last part of the big data definition is velocity. Velocity describes the ever-growing amount of big data. In the digital era, data is expected to grow exponentially, and it is often perceived to be very hard for companies to catch up with this enormous speed. However, velocity ensures that the data can be analysed in real-time and is able to support businesses with their decision-making processes (Huang et al., 2017, p. 1229). Nevertheless, sometimes the 3V-concept may be extended by other characteristics such as veracity (referring to the authenticity of big data) and value (Mohanta, Nanda, & Patnaik, 2020, p. 5). In order to actually extract the mentioned value from big data, sophisticated and advanced technologies have to be taken into place. Different business intelligence tools, being further examined in *chapter 2.2.2*, assist companies with processing and analysing the huge datasets being available. Having said this, big data is only helpful, if companies understand how to work with it and know exactly how to gain valuable insights within the business intelligence process (Rabhi et al., 2019, pp. 599–600).

2.2.2 BUSINESS INTELLIGENCE TOOLS

After having harvested and stored the large amount of data being available to a company, it is important to choose the right business intelligence tools in order to analyse the data given properly. Having said this, it is crucial that companies know the different tools being feasible. This ensures that a profound decision on which tools actual fulfil the company's needs best and bring the desired results for their individual purposes can be made. Hereby, it has to be mentioned, that there is a huge variety of different business intelligence tools available on the market (Pribisalić, Jugo, & Martinčić-Ipšić, 2019, p. 447). During the past years, several firms have invested large amounts of money into the development of advanced business intelligence technologies which again underlines their high value in strategic business processes (Grublješič & Jaklič, 2015, p. 300). Having said this, it may be hard for companies, especially unexperienced ones, to choose among the variety of technologies being on the market (Datapine, 2020). After the choice has been made, it is crucial for businesses to constantly evaluate their business intelligence tools in order to make sure that they are always using state-of-the-art technologies. This helps companies to ensure the ability to stay competitive with other businesses using the same business intelligence technologies (Wauyo, Omol, & Okumu, 2017, p. 60). Another aspect that has to be considered, is that business intelligence tools are often coming with different basic and/or advanced features. It has to be regarded that especially the advanced business intelligence tools may not offer companies the possibility to use rather basic features such as ad-hoc reports, key performance indicators, or other performance metrics. Due to this aspect companies should be aware that a compromise between the cutting-edge functionalities and the actual broadness of a business intelligence tool may be indispensable (Pribisalić, Jugo, & Martinčić-Ipšić, 2019, p. 448). Having said this, one advanced feature of a lot of business intelligence tools is big data analytics. This technology is used to analyse, link, and compare a vast number of data sets (Dremel et al., 2020, p.

1). Moreover, it helps companies to use business intelligence for uncovering different correlations and patterns and extracting useful knowledge out of the large data sets being available. Generally speaking, big data analytics combines different analysis practices such as data mining, predictive analysis, and machine learning in order to understand a company's customers better, drive innovation, and optimise different business processes. Furthermore, big data analytics can be applied among many different industries, such as telecommunication, retail, or healthcare in order to drive value for their respective business activities (Huang et al., 2017, p. 1230).

However, it has to be considered that business intelligence features, such as big data analytics, still require the existence of working professionals with the possession of different data analytical skills in order to actually use the business intelligence technologies appropriately. Concerning the future of business intelligence technologies, it is perceived to be shaped by a new approach, the so-called augmented analysis. This technology is mainly integrating the concept of artificial intelligence. Furthermore, this new business intelligence tool mainly uses machine-learning and natural language processing for the automation of data analysis and further distribution of insights for supporting the organisational decision-making processes. It is predicted that augmented analytics is likely to outperform current data scientists as it is seemingly taking over all their respective daily business tasks (Abas et al., 2020, pp. 3561–3562). In addition, augmented analytics is assumed to enhance the comprehensive business intelligence user experience with the transformation of data analytics into something very intuitive and comprehensive (Pribisalić, Jugo, & Martinčić-Ipšić, 2019, p. 450).

2.2.3 DATA-DRIVEN AND NEEDS-DRIVEN DECISION-MAKING

After the vast amount of data sets have been analysed and visualised thoroughly, a certain decision-making is taking place (Smith, 2020, p. 44). The increasing importance of business intelligence in the economy has led to a correspondently raising awareness for decision-making processes that are based on useful data sets. Having said this, this idea forced the development of two different approaches arising in the decision-making context of business intelligence: The first one is data-driven decision-making. By using this approach, companies identify the overall availability of data and its related analysis results as their main drivers to use business intelligence technologies. This decision-making method implies that businesses are gaining several insights through business intelligence technologies without having any expectations or requirements concerning the data analysis results (Skyrius et al., 2016, pp. 174–175). Data-driven decision-making is said to rely solely on the data insights presented and refrains from implementing intuition into the decision-making process. Furthermore, it has been proven that companies, following the data-driven approach, are improving their overall business performance relatively to their applied degree of data-based judgements (Provost & Fawcett, 2013, p. 53).

The other decision-making method is the so-called needs-driven approach. Even though data is still the most important decision determinant, this approach focuses on driving business intelligence by highlighting the primary role of well-thought of and well-pointed business questions, being demanded to the specific data available. Companies have evolved the need to generate certain business insights and hence, business intelligence is used in a whole different way than with the data-driven approach. It can be said that needs-driven decision-making is mainly associated with a certain need or problem arising through a complex situation. Accordingly, this need has to be answered by different business intelligence insights (Skyrius et al., 2016, pp. 174–175). The general aim of the needs-driven approach is to place accurate business questions before executing business intelligence in order to have a certain framework to work with. As a consequence, a company is able to know very precisely which information they want to extract instead of analysing everything and hoping that the desired answers to their key business questions will be delivered by chance. Therefore, with this decision-making approach, business intelligence technologies are actively used to find solutions for existing or designed problems.

The technologies have to ensure to bridge the divide between business intelligence insights and their actual business value and application (Troyanos, 2020).

2.3 Business intelligence agility, maturity, and acceptance

The purpose of this chapter is to examine the highly relevant business intelligence determinants: business intelligence agility, business intelligence maturity, and business intelligence acceptance. Moreover, related aspects and theories are highlighted.

2.3.1 Business intelligence agility

In the digital era, a growing interest in being as flexible as possible is occurring. Having said this, business intelligence plays a huge role in supporting the so-called dynamic capabilities approach. The usage of business intelligence helps companies to shape their sustainable survival strategies by creating dynamic capabilities or competencies, assisted by the usage of information technologies. In addition, it has to be mentioned that those dynamic capabilities should be unique and hard to be replicated by other companies (Skyrius et al., 2016, p. 176). In this context, the theory of gaining competitive advantage through information by Michael E. Porter and Victor E. Millar applies. The theory states that companies are able to remodel their products or services created by using the gained information insights properly. Furthermore, information has proven to affect every step along the value chain and hence, aims to maximise value for the customers in every business process. Information is able to optimise possible trade-offs that may occur through the linkages between the different business processes, as they are likely to affect each other's performance significantly (Porter & Millar, 1985, pp. 150–152). Moreover, it has to be emphasised that value creation and competitive advantage through information or business intelligence can only be achieved, if the employees of a company are actually able and willing to apply the information gained accordingly (Koch & Windsperger, 2017, p. 8). This aspect is going to be further examined in *chapter 2.3.3*. Generally speaking, the dynamic capabilities approach combines business intelligence with the underlying theory of Porter and Millar. Hence, business intelligence agility is achieved, when the most important intangible asset of a company is able to reconfigure itself whenever the ever-changing business environment creates the need for it. Having said this, business intelligence agility is mostly referring to the internal intelligence of businesses and tends to follow the needs-driven approach, being examined in *chapter 2.2.3*. It is of high importance, that business intelligence systems can react to required changes in real-time and are able to foresee potential changes coming in the future by analysing former events sufficiently. This specific agility aims to perform with minimal costs in order to support the business survival strategies chosen properly (Knapke & Olbrich, 2016, p. 4). As a consequence, business intelligence systems have to be highly automated, constantly accessible, unified throughout the whole organisation, and not limited by outdated technology in order to actually be agile (Skyrius et al., 2016, pp. 176–177).

2.3.2 BUSINESS INTELLIGENCE MATURITY

Another very important part of business intelligence is its degree of maturity. Maturity can be defined as the description of "a very advanced or developed form or state" (Cambridge University Press, 2020). Transferred to the world of business intelligence, this means that maturity models are needed in order to transform a company or business unit from an initial state to the targeted maturity state with the assistance of business intelligence systems (Shaaban et al., 2012, p. 277). Moreover, in order to maximise the specific benefits of business intelligence, it is crucial for companies to understand that the business intelligence maturity within the company has to match the general maturity degree of the organisation as such (Rajterič, 2010, p. 48). Furthermore, the usage of business intelligence maturity models supports businesses in evaluating their current performance and realising an enhanced decision-making process (Shaaban et al., 2012, p. 276). Having said this, business intelligence maturity models are able to measure the influence of business intelligence on an organisation as a whole. Even though there are a lot of different maturity models in the area of business intelligence, all of them have one in common: they are based on the concept of a constantly changing environment and assume that those changes can be predicted and coordinated. As a consequence, business intelligence maturity models are able to characterise, analyse, and evaluate the growth lifecycles of different business areas. Through the usage of maturity models, companies are able to align their different information systems accordingly to their actual business efforts. Furthermore, those maturity models help companies to figure out their current state of performance and help to realise how they need to change in order to improve the overall business performance. In this context, it has to be mentioned that the level of maturity within the different organisations is highly individual, depending on their actual level of business intelligence usage (Rajterič, 2010, pp. 49–50). Having said this, the underlying concept of a business intelligence maturity model is demonstrated on the example of the Gartner's business intelligence and performance management maturity model:

Figure 2   Business intelligence and performance management maturity model

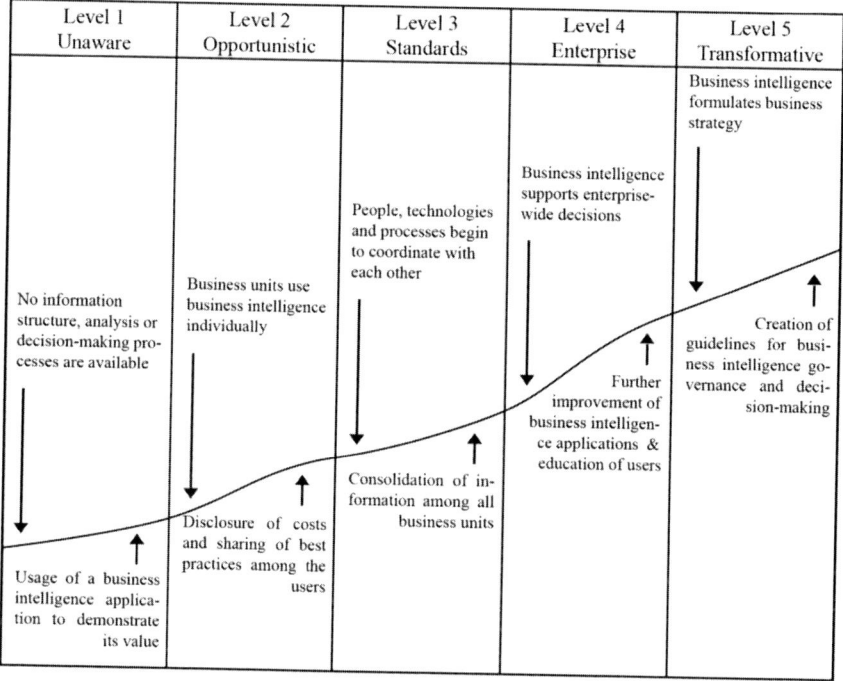

Note: own illustration, based on Hostmann & Hagerty, 2010, pp. 2-5.

2.3.3 BUSINESS INTELLIGENCE ACCEPTANCE

The opportunities coming along with the integration of business intelligence systems can only be realised to their full potentials, if the respective technology is actually accepted and supported throughout the whole organisation. That is why it is tremendously important for companies to prevent low acceptance levels among the users of business intelligence, as this might hinder its subsequent success (Grublješič & Jaklič, 2015, p. 299).

Moreover, the degree of acceptability of companies towards business intelligence systems is stated to mirror the strategic creditability of an organisation throughout all conducted business processes (Arefin, Hoque, & Bao, 2015, p. 280). In this context, different models and theories have evolved in order to find specific reasons for people's perceptions and utilisations of technological systems. Having said this, one way to explain business intelligence acceptance is the technology acceptance model. This acceptance theory deals with several internal and external variables, influencing people's degree of usage of technology. These determinants are for example the perceived usefulness, self-efficacy, attitude towards technology, and subjective norms (Scherer, Siddiq, & Tondeur, 2019, pp. 13–14). The underlying theory of the technology acceptance model is the social psychological approach "of predicting behavioural intentions and actual behaviour" (Grublješič & Jaklič, 2015, p. 300). This approach is said to combine the two theories of reasoned action and planned behaviour by Fishbein & Ajzen. As a consequence, the technology acceptance model explains that business intelligence acceptance is a combination of the realised ease of use and usefulness of a technology and the actual underlying intention of its usage (Grublješič & Jaklič, 2015, p. 300). The concept of the technology acceptance model has been highly discussed in research and has proven to be the "leading model in predicting system use" (Chuttur, 2009, p. 2).

2.4 OPPORTUNITIES FOR COMPANIES

Business intelligence offers companies a variety of opportunities that have to be outlined in the context of this research. First of all, the integration of business intelligence helps to bring an order into the vast amount of data being collected (Purnamasari et al., 2019, p. 1). By storing and processing the different data harvested, companies are able to get a better picture of which information is actually available to them and what currently is happening within their organisation (Durcevic, 2018). Furthermore, business intelligence is the solution to the economy-wide problem of having too many data sets and not knowing how to store, deal, and use them properly. Business intelligence is able to provide accurate information to different departments within the organisation at the right time and via the right channel (Aufaure et al., 2015, p. 101). Moreover, the different business intelligence tools make it possible for companies to access valuable data in real-time, ensuring that a company is always up-to-date and able to stay flexible in its operations. Additionally, those tools are able to visualise the insights gained for information spread throughout the whole company. As a consequence, employees who are not data scientists are able to use the data processed for their different business purposes (Pribisalić, Jugo, & Martinčić-Ipšić, 2019, pp. 444–445).

Having said this, business intelligence technologies are able to identify trends early, forecast several scenarios, and help businesses to ensure a sustainable decision-making process throughout the whole company (Purnamasari et al., 2019, p. 2). Additionally, business intelligence technologies are often designed to register "early warning signals of danger from unexpected sources" (Frates & Sharp, 2005, p. 17). Another opportunity that business intelligence offers companies is the gain of a better customer knowledge. It helps companies to learn about their customers and their purchasing behaviours thoroughly, as well as building better relationships with the existing customers through valid information systems (Purnamasari et al., 2019, p. 2). Furthermore, the better understanding of a company's existing customers can also lead to the discovery of new customer segments. This may often result in obtaining new market opportunities (Frates & Sharp, 2005, p. 17). Due to the leveraging of big data and resulting support in several decision-making processes, companies are able to increase their return on investments in different business fields with the usage of business intelligence systems (Williams, 2016, p. 17). This often leads to a sustainable reduction of costs. Furthermore, business intelligence can be seen as an extension to the current business strategy of an organisation while being simultaneously able to shape the respective actions of the future. Having said this, it is able to support different strategic processes, resulting in the achievement of competitive advantage through information, being further described in *chapter 2.3.1* (Wauyo, Omol, & Okumu, 2017, pp. 61–62). In addition to that, especially the process of internationalisation can be supported by the accurate integration of business intelligence technologies. The predictive detection of available opportunities in an often very turbulent market environment can help businesses to enter foreign markets more easily. In this context, business intelligence is able to guide companies with the provision of extensive information about the host markets, potential competitors, and governmental regulations so that a profound and promising internationalisation strategy can be developed (Cheng, Zhong, & Cao, 2020, p. 96). As business intelligence is conceptualised to be used throughout a whole organisation, an enhanced collaboration, communication, and information sharing between the different business departments is executed. This often results in improved problem-solving processes. Through the constant backup of information and knowledge in the data warehouses, transparency and control over essential business processes can be guaranteed. Furthermore, business intelligence helps companies to have a comprehensible information base in case any criticism regarding several management decisions from the past may arise (Gluchowski, Gabriel, & Dittmar, 2008, pp. 355–356). Another advantage of business intelligence would be that it is not limited to one specific industry only. The concept is widely applicable among all types of businesses dealing with big data and its relatives. Regardless of the industry, the business intelligence technologies are able to adapt to the individual needs of the different companies. Examples for the different sectors using business intelligence would be the healthcare, banking, telecommunication, and manufacturing branches (Arefin, Hoque, & Bao, 2015, p. 264).

2.5 CHALLENGES FOR COMPANIES

After highlighting the opportunities of business intelligence for companies, it is of high importance to have a closer look at the potential challenges coming along with its implementation. Hereby, it has to be considered, that one key challenge can be identified: the integration of employees into the business intelligence process. Apart from the technical aspects, the human factors being necessary for the accurate integration of business intelligence systems have to be considered. Even though some companies may have already understood that business intelligence systems have to rely on technical and human factors equally, most companies are still forgetting to include their lower-level managers and employees into the process of business intelligence. This leads to a lot of sub-challenges emerging (Skyrius et al., 2016, p. 173):

First of all, the potential and value of business intelligence cannot be fully realised throughout the whole company. Often, only the superior managers are understanding the urge and opportunities that business intelligence offers, but the lower-level managers and employees (who are the core users of the technologies) cannot relate. It is very likely that they are not informed enough and hence not able to project the high value of business intelligence onto their current and future needs or business application fields (Gluchowski, Gabriel, & Dittmar, 2008, p. 356). As a consequence, employees might still extract data (from different sources) on their own and produce subjective results for their own needs while the sophisticated business intelligence systems are running simultaneously. Employees might not feel the urge to share information throughout the company, which often leads to unnecessary effort duplication and results being hard to validate afterwards. Furthermore, companies might not understand that the integration of business intelligence systems does not mean that they have a static reporting tool being suitable for a lifetime usage. In addition, business intelligence is an ever-changing system that constantly adapts to the technological trends and business needs. Having said this, not only the business intelligence systems have to be agile, but the users (mostly lower-level managers and employees) have to be open to an agile working approach, as well (Skyrius et al., 2016, pp. 172–173). Another key challenge that has to be considered, is that a common education and terminology has to be introduced throughout the whole organisation in order to make the users understand what is really helpful and what is just a temporary hype. Furthermore, this helps the users to clearly identify how to actually leverage the available data for business improvement purposes (Williams, 2016, p. 27). In addition, it has proven to be very difficult for companies to share a common mindset and understanding regarding business intelligence technologies, as the different terms involved are often subject to various definitions and meanings. Moreover, different departments have to share the same knowledge about business intelligence in order to be able to extract its full potential. The last aspect which is often a common failure of companies using business intelligence systems, is the risk of making mistakes as a consequence of wanting to reduce costs to the bare minimum. This approach often leads to the integration of several inaccurate and inflexible third-party business intelligence technologies. It has to be emphasised that business intelligence is a framework that should not be subject to outsourcing as this does not align with the main purpose of its application and harms its highly strategic function tremendously (Skyrius et al., 2016, p. 173). Furthermore, it has to be regarded that the aforementioned threats have to be taken into careful consideration before deciding on whether or not integrating business intelligence into the corporate culture.

By minimising the previously stated sub-challenges, companies are able to make sure that the core of the company, its employees, are well-trained and able to actually extract valuable information out of business intelligence systems. With this approach they will be able to gain the desired competitive advantage and maximise their overall business results (Williams, 2016, p. 18).

3 AFFILIATE MARKETING

This chapter is dedicated to the online marketing tool affiliate marketing. It examines its definition, differentiates it from other online marketing tools, shows basic functional elements and highlights its general importance and relationship to the travel industry.

3.1 DEFINITION AND DIFFERENTIATION

Generally speaking, *affiliate marketing* is an approach being used to market one's product or service in the digital world (Patrick & Hee, 2019, p. 703). It is defined as an Internet-based tool that has the aim to distribute products or services and generate sales while communicating actively with the different customers. Furthermore, it has to be mentioned that this online marketing approach has proven to come with very little financial risk for all parties being involved (Bormann, 2019, p. 21). As a consequence, it is one of the most popular online marketing instruments (Chachra, Savage, & Voelker, 2015, p. 41). Moreover, affiliate marketing is one of the oldest online marketing practices, as it is originating in the mid 1990s. Even though a lot of people accredit Amazon founder Jeff Bezos for the invention of affiliate marketing, it has actually been developed by William J. Tobin in 1994. The founder of an online platform designed a specific framework of tracking and compensating sales successfully, being patented in 1996. However, even though the invention of affiliate marketing is nothing Amazon can be accounted for, it can be said that the company owns the oldest active affiliate programme in the world (Bormann, 2019, p. 21). In fact, Amazon has managed to select affiliate marketing as their main business model and it reached about 60,000 registered partners on their website within the first year of operating (Lammenett, 2019, p. 63). Having said this, the functional principle of affiliate marketing is further explained in the subsequent *chapter 3.2.1*.

As different online marketing practices have emerged during the last decades (Bormann, 2019, p. 131), it is highly important to differentiate the practice of affiliate marketing from the other online marketing channels existing. Especially the practise of display advertising could be mixed up with affiliate marketing easily, as both digital marketing practices include the usage of banners as means of advertising (Kundenwachstum.de, 2020). Display advertisements are either text- or image-based and distributed on a variety of different websites, mobile or video applications. Those display advertising partners are usually part of a special display advertising network. Additionally, the underlying concept of this digital marketing tool is that the different advertisements are only displayed on the aforementioned platforms, if the related content of the partners is fitting to the purpose of the display marketing campaigns (Bahga & Madisetti, 2019, p. 28). Another online marketing discipline that has to be differentiated is the approach of influencer marketing. This online marketing channel can be seen as an extension to affiliate marketing (Perret & Edler, 2018, p. 12) and is used to promote a company's product or service with the use of individuals. The main characteristic of these individuals is that they are having a high reach on social media platforms, such as Instagram. The influencers chosen are perceived as experts from their specific target groups or followers and, as a consequence, function as referrals with the aim to drive the traffic and sales figures of a company. As a matter of fact, influencer marketing is relatively new and highly related to the established affiliate marketing (Perret & Edler, 2018, p. 12; Shirisha, 2018, p. 613). Having said this, both disciplines should not be mistaken for one another.

3.2 FUNDAMENTALS OF AFFILIATE MARKETING

The aim of this chapter is to outline the fundamentals of the online marketing channel affiliate marketing and show its complexity in terms of the different actors being involved and options to choose. These options refer to affiliate networks, commission models, and tracking methods. Furthermore, potential affiliate fraud scenarios and corresponding prevention measures are examined.

3.2.1 FUNCTIONAL PRINCIPLE

Generally speaking, affiliate marketing is nothing that had to be newly invented, as it simply transfers the traditional merchant-distributor mechanism of the offline world into the digital environment (Lammenett, 2019, p. 63). The aim of affiliate marketing is to distribute the merchants' products and services via several Internet-partners, the so-called publishers or affiliates, in order to reach as many (potential) customers as possible (Bormann, 2019, p. 22). In affiliate marketing, a performance-based remuneration concept is applied which leads to a correlation between the publishers' performance during the affiliate campaign and the actual commission fee being paid to the affiliate (Libai, Biyalogorsky, & Gerstner, 2003, p. 305). This win-win situation is mainly determined by a certain commission model being individually negotiated by the merchant and affiliate (Lammenett, 2019, p. 63). Having said this, the most common commission models can be found in *chapter 3.2.3*. In this context, it has to be emphasised that affiliate marketing involves three main actors: a merchant, a publisher, and the user. However, there is always the possibility to involve a forth actor, an affiliate network, into the process (Petersen, 2017, p. 330). This is going to be further examined in *chapter 3.2.2*. The first affiliate marketing actor that has to be mentioned is the merchant or so-called advertiser. He is the driving force that is initiating the process of affiliate marketing for a respective company. After that the merchant actively chooses a partner to work with and aims to increase the company's website traffic with the redirection of traffic from the affiliate partners' website(s) (Bala & Verma, 2018, p. 332). This can be realised by the integration of specific means of advertising such as text links, banners, buttons, product feeds or videos on the affiliates' website (Lammenett, 2019, pp. 77–80). Having said this, in order to gain more website traffic and build a virtual structure of distribution, a merchant needs to have reliable partners (Olbrich, Schultz, & Holsing, 2019, p. 128). These partners are the so-called publishers or affiliates – the second actor being involved in the process of affiliate marketing. A publisher is further characterised as the owner of a website, offering different kinds of content to its users. In this context, it has to be mentioned, that not every website owner can monetise his website and be part of the affiliate marketing process. Different professional groups such as lawyers, doctors, or public institutions are under obligation to be neutral in either way. As a consequence, the participation in affiliate networks of any kind is prohibited by law (Bormann, 2019, p. 22). Having said this, due to the popularity of affiliate marketing, a lot of different affiliate business models have evolved. A vast number of publishers have set their focus on one specific affiliate branch in order to provide the desired content to the different website visitor groups. Moreover, the most common affiliate categories are content publishers (e.g., blogs), deal publishers (reporting on general deals), coupon publishers (offering exclusive coupons), cashback publishers (offering cashback in different forms for users shopping via their affiliate links), and comparison publishers (listing similar products of different brands in order to show the user the most suitable offer) (Petersen, 2017, p. 333). In addition, it is of huge importance that the affiliate partner chosen and his respective affiliate business model fit to the products or services of the merchant, in order to share a common user interest (Middleton et al., 2009, p. 263). However, all of the aforementioned means could not lead to a successful online marketing technique, if the third affiliate marketing actor, the user, would not interact with the affiliate partners. By visiting a publisher's website and clicking on an affiliation advertisement displayed, the user is redirected to the merchant's website. On this website, the user gets the possibility to get further information about the merchants' products or services (Olbrich, Schultz, & Holsing, 2019, p. 113). In an ideal scenario, this website visit will then lead to the predefined affiliate campaign objective. This might be, for example, the conversion into a valuable customer (Zimmermann, 2011, p. 294).

Figure 3 Illustration of the affiliate marketing principle

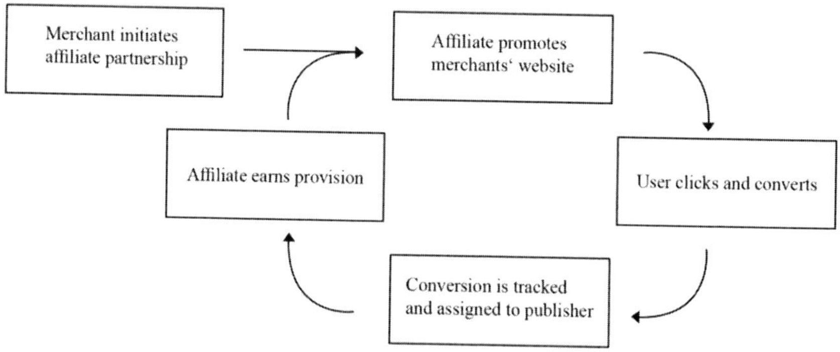

```
Merchant initiates            Affiliate promotes
affiliate partnership   →     merchants' website

                                    ↓
Affiliate earns provision     User clicks and converts

         ↑
         Conversion is tracked
         and assigned to publisher
```

Note: own illustration

3.2.2 EXTERNAL AFFILIATE NETWORK VS. IN-HOUSE AFFILIATE NETWORK

Having examined the functional principle of affiliate marketing, the bigger picture has to be regarded. Depending on the size of the merchant's company and corresponding product range, two different options of managing the affiliate marketing channel occur: working with an existing, external affiliate network or setting up an affiliate network on one's own and manage its function in-house (Bangari, Panwar, & Thakur, 2019, p. 131). Speaking about the external affiliate networks, there are several advantages that have to be highlighted. First of all, the networks are likely to have a large number of already registered publishers which makes it very easy for merchants, being new in the affiliate marketing game, to get in touch with a variety of publishers from different sectors (Lammenett, 2019, p. 68). Furthermore, the management of the application and acquisition process can be conducted easily, as the networks are likely to have specific mechanisms being intentionally implemented for these purposes (Duffy, 2005,

p. 162). In order to make the merchant-publisher relationship as comfortable as possible, affiliate networks provide the merchant with a ready-to-use technology and tracking set-up that is guaranteeing an accountable sales distribution among the different publishers (Olbrich, Schultz, & Bormann, 2019, p. 48). Due to these well-developed technologies, the affiliate networks are able to calculate the publisher commissions precisely and take care of the billing processes as such (Amarasekara, 2016, p. 1). Another advantage of external affiliate networks is, that the legal framework is already given and publisher contracts of any kind are instantly available (Lammenett, 2019, p. 71).

Coming to the downside of external affiliate networks, it has to be highlighted, that not every affiliate network is suitable for every merchant. A lot of external affiliate networks tend to have several strategic positionings like, for example, different thematic approaches. Moreover, the size of an affiliate network is crucial for maximising the merchants' chance to enter the affiliate market in the best way possible. That is why merchants have to know the potential affiliate networks very well in order to come to a sustainable and profitable network decision (Lammenett, 2019, p. 83). Additionally, due to the popularity of external affiliate networks, the entry barriers can be rather high and there is always the probability that a merchant will not be accepted by a network. It is common that affiliate networks select only merchants that are associated with a high probability of generating great revenues. This shows that the external affiliate networks' own intention of earning as much commission as possible is often determining their respective merchant approvals (Lammenett, 2019, p. 68). Another disadvantage would be the general costs coming along with external affiliate networks. In order to be accepted and onboarded by an affiliate network, merchants often have to pay a one-time admission fee. This fee is said to be calculated on the basis of the size and rating of the merchant and hence, may alter between 2,000 and 5,000 euros (Lammenett, 2015, p. 75). Furthermore, merchants have to pay additional network fees, being billed on a permanent basis. Those affiliate network fees are related to the publisher remunerations, as merchants are obliged to pay the networks a certain percentage of the net publisher fee. Still, this payment is said to compensate the management of the daily affiliate business activities, being absorbed by the external affiliate networks (Prussakov, 2011, p. 52).

Regarding the second affiliate marketing approach, the creation of an in-house affiliate network, one huge advantage has to be highlighted. With the integration of this approach, merchants are not obligated to pay any additional fee to a third party and a pure merchant-publisher relationship can be established (Lammenett, 2019, p. 68). Having said this, the challenges of setting up an in-house affiliate network autonomously, are perceived to be predominant. In order to get in touch with potential publishers, the merchant has to put extra effort in the self-marketing of the own affiliate network and company brand. Publishers are unlikely to find the respective merchant on their own, as the company is not part of a well-known and established network. In addition, the publisher acquisition has to be maintained proactively, resulting in a lot of work for the merchant. Having said this, as soon as a merchant is able to acquire a publisher for its in-house affiliate network, the next obstacle is arising: a legal framework for the merchant-publisher relationship has to be developed carefully and certified by a notary public. This does not only require a certain degree of legal expertise, but also comes along with certain additional costs for the services of the notary public. Another disadvantage of this affiliate network approach would be that the tracking technologies have to be developed by the merchant himself or bought and integrated by third parties. This is not only very time-consuming but can also be very costly for the merchant. Last but not least, the merchant has to execute the billing process manually, which can be very complex depending on how many publishers have been onboarded (Lammenett, 2019, pp. 68–71).

3.2.3 COMMISSION MODELS

As mentioned in *chapter 3.2.1*, there are several models underlying the process of commissioning in affiliate marketing. However, it can be said that the most common models used are pay per click, pay per lead and pay per sale (Lammenett, 2019, p. 63). Furthermore, the commission model is said to be chosen by the merchant initiating the affiliation (Olbrich, Schultz, & Bormann, 2019, p. 48). First of all, the concept of pay per click has to be examined. This approach refers to a commission being paid for every customer that is redirected from the affiliate's to the merchant's website. With this payment option, the merchant solely pays for the traffic being generated through the publisher. As a consequence, subsequent user actions will not be taken into consideration when calculating the affiliate provision (Dwivedi, Rana, & Alryalat, 2017, p. 35). Having said this, the affiliate compensation in the pay per click model is likely to range between 0.03 and 0.25 euros per click. Due to its characteristic of easily being subject to fraud, this payment model has proven to be the least favourite of the three presented. The next commonly used payment model is pay per lead. Here, the merchant compensates the affiliate partner for every lead being generated through its affiliation activities. Furthermore, this model is likely to be chosen by merchants whose products cannot be bought directly on their website or are classified as intangible products (Lammenett, 2019, pp. 74–75). Having said this, pay per lead refers to every trackable user contact being acquired through affiliation processes. This is mainly subject to actions such as newsletter subscriptions or starting a download (Unternehmer.de, 2020). In addition, pay per lead is remunerated with a fixed amount per lead, being subject to variability and depending on the previous negotiations that have been made. However, the amount per lead is stated to be usually determined by the merchant's business model. Insurance companies, dating services, or financial services have shown to prefer this approach of commissioning in affiliate marketing (Lammenett, 2019, pp. 74–75). The last payment concept, pay per sale, refers to the publisher being remunerated for every sale that is generated through its redirection to the merchant's website. It is known as the most common provisioning practice of all. Having said this, pay per sale is a very specific modification of the pay per action model, where any action conducted is commissioned (Dwivedi, Rana, & Alryalat, 2017, p. 35). In contrast to the previously presented commission models, pay per sale is not measured in fixed amounts per action, but calculated on a certain percentage base. This means that affiliates are compensated with a percentage of the net revenue generated by every customer that has been acquired through their affiliation actions (Wandiger, 2020). Having said this, it has to be emphasised that there is the additional possibility to negotiate mixed commission models. It is advised that merchants choose the remuneration approaches accordingly to their business models in order to be able to fulfil the previously set affiliate campaign objectives successfully (Lammenett, 2019, p. 77). However, regardless of the commission model chosen, the affiliates are paid as soon as the predefined objective of the campaign cannot be revised anymore. This is usually subject to the individual revocation periods of the merchants' products or services. Having said this, it is common practice that commissions are likely to be paid after a period of 14 days (Deges, 2020, p. 170).

3.2.4 Tracking methods and affiliate fraud

In order to guarantee an appropriate commission fee calculation for the publishers and monitor the correlated performance properly, external affiliate networks (if the merchant chooses to bring in a third party into the affiliation process) or the merchant himself have to make sure that a credible tracking solution is implemented sufficiently. The objective of the tracking implementation is to validate the sales, leads or clicks being generated by the different affiliation activities (Edelman & Brandi, 2015, p. 2). However, as examined in *chapter 3.2.2*, this can either be in the hands of the merchant (choosing to do an in-house affiliate network) or in the hands of the external affiliate network that the merchant has chosen to partner with. Regardless of which affiliate network option is chosen, a wide range of tracking methods can be applied. This would be, for example, URL tracking, cookie tracking, session tracking, database tracking, or pixel tracking. However, all of these different tracking methods have the common aim of identifying and assigning a website visitor and its corresponding conversion or lead to a certain affiliate. Depending on the different requirements the tracking method has to fulfil, the merchant and/or external affiliate network choose one of the abovementioned tracking approaches (Lammenett, 2007, p. 26). In this context it has to be mentioned, that all tracking methods are used for the purpose of click and conversion tracking. Because of this, the click tracking is perceived to record every click through which a user has been redirected to the merchant's website. The conversion tracking, on the other hand, reports as soon as this user has generated a predefined conversion or lead. If the tracking system records a successful conversion via the conversion tracking but no correspondent click activity can be retraced, the conversion will not be accounted to the particular publisher. This guarantees that no commission is being paid for users that enter the website via a direct URL type-in or other forms of online marketing (Amarasekara, 2016, pp. 11–12). Due to the different laws in the field of data privacy, such as the *General Data Protection Regulation (GDPR)*, and individual sentences, the tracking process in affiliate marketing is a very sensible and highly discussed topic. Especially the cookie tracking method and its associated need for consent through the user is in the spotlight, as it has to be wisely conducted in order to prevent violations of the existing laws and legal practices. As a consequence, affiliate marketers have to be very careful in their decision-making of which tracking method to choose and how to actually implement it (Kellermann, 2019). As the tracking process is essentially responsible for the calculation of the affiliate commissions (Bormann, 2019, p. 58), this part of the affiliate marketing process is often subject to different affiliate fraud approaches (Edelman & Brandi, 2015, p. 3). With the passage of time, a variety of fraudulent affiliate marketing activities, mainly targeting the cookie-based tracking processes, have emerged. All these different methods have one common aim: they try to manipulate the tracking processes by inserting inaccurate transaction information (Amarasekara & Mathrani, 2016, p. 1). Having said this, one type of affiliate fraud is the so-called cookie stuffing (Amarasekara, 2016, p. 14). By setting cookies for a user who has not actively clicked on a certain affiliation link, fraudulent publishers aim to earn commissions for possible transactions that do not originally emerge out of their affiliation activities. This type of fraud is very likely to appear, when affiliates are integrating the different means of advertising via an Iframe (Denzin, 2019, p. 30), meaning a coded element being used to incorporate different means of advertising of third parties (Onlinemarketing-Praxis, 2020). Apart from that cookie stuffing can be prevented by the progressive monitoring of the different affiliation activities conducted and an active questioning of the details of every related transaction (Denzin, 2019, p. 30).

In this context, another type of fraud has to be considered: the affiliate hopping. Affiliate hopping is a certain type of affiliate fraud that is based on the publisher partnering with the same merchant on different affiliate networks. As affiliate networks are perceived to work independently and hence, no further exchange of information is taking place, affiliate partners, who have the intention of fraud, aim at manipulating the tracking technologies of these independent affiliate networks. As a consequence, the affiliate will get paid on both networks for one accomplished transaction, so that the publisher is charged twice. This can be easily prevented by a sufficient observation of the different affiliate marketing transactions and further possible cancellations in the process (Olbrich, Schultz, & Holsing, 2019, p. 131). Another affiliate fraud method is the execution of transactions on the merchants' website with the usage of false customer information. In this case, fraudulent affiliate partners speculate that the merchant does not validate the different transactions and related customer information properly, so that an unauthorised provision is being paid. It can be said, that affiliate campaigns with the objective of lead generation are mainly subject to this type of affiliate fraud (Bormann, 2019, p. 71). This double-commissioning can be prevented by the careful validation of transaction- or lead information by the merchant. Furthermore, the merchant has to make sure that the commissions are only being paid after a certain period of time, so that a decisive transaction or lead has evidently succeeded (Olbrich, Schultz, & Holsing, 2019, p. 132).

3.3 IMPORTANCE OF AFFILIATE MARKETING

This chapter includes an overview of the opportunities that affiliate marketing offers companies. Furthermore, the overall value of affiliate marketing in the online marketing mix is outlined.

3.3.1 OPPORTUNITIES FOR COMPANIES

Affiliate marketing is not only perceived as a great opportunity for companies to increase their overall traffic and, consequently, sales or leads, it has also proven to be an online marketing channel that is having very low administrative costs. Due to the performance-based model underlying the concept of affiliate marketing, companies are able to lower their financial risks and wastages while achieving a good return on investment. Moreover, companies indirectly benefit of the overall drive of the publishers to promote their affiliate websites to a highly valuable customer base. Due to the performance-based remuneration, affiliates are aiming to maximise their own remuneration by these additional promotions. As a consequence, this automatically leads to the corresponding maximisation of the merchants' revenues during the run of an affiliate campaign (Gregori, Daniele, & Altinay, 2014, p. 197). Another benefit of affiliate marketing would be that it creates further, external touchpoints along the customer journey. The cooperation with a variety of different affiliate partners enables a lot of virtual touchpoints with the merchants' brand. As a consequence, the brand perception of a company is enhanced and the merchants' website is accordingly gaining in popularity. Having said this, businesses have to pay attention to the different publisher characteristics, such as their main target group and image, in order to guarantee a valuable traffic redirection (Deges, 2020, pp. 160–168). In addition, affiliate marketing offers companies the opportunity to integrate their means of advertising in a variety of ways, such as integrated or link-based solutions. This results in the possibility of integrating affiliation activities into, for example, the shopping baskets of affiliate partners. Furthermore, it may ensure a nearly seamless integration of the merchants' offers in different content articles (Kollmann, Suckow, & Peschl, 2015, p. 170). Having said this, affiliate marketing does not only help companies to maximise their revenues, but it also gives the chance to build credibility regarding their overall brand image (Suchada et al., 2017, p. 132). In this context, it is tremendously important for companies to choose publishers wisely in order to support the existing brand image and protect oneself from a negative brand perception caused by third parties (Kollmann, Suckow, & Peschl, 2015, p. 170). Furthermore, the publishers are able to target a specific audience efficiently, as they are likely to "have a strong understanding of their average visitor profile" (Gregori, Daniele, & Altinay, 2014, p. 197). This helps the companies to get a better understanding of their actual target group and makes it possible to harvest real-time data about important market research topics, such as buying behaviours or existing consumer trends (Gregori, Daniele, & Altinay, 2014, pp. 197–198). Another benefit of this online marketing tool is that, due to the increased number of external links through affiliation activities, the merchants' website is likely to achieve a better ranking and visibility on the search engine results pages. As a consequence, affiliate marketing has proven to have a positive and sustainable impact on the merchants' overall website performance (Daniele et al., 2009, p. 347). However, it has to be mentioned that affiliate marketing can only unfold its full potential when it is part of an integrated online marketing strategy. Here, it may take advantage of the benefits of other online marketing channels and potential synergies (Kärner, 2016). This aspect is going to be further examined in the subsequent *chapter 3.3.2*.

3.3.2 AFFILIATE MARKETING IN THE OVERALL ONLINE MARKETING MIX

As a consequence of the ever-ongoing digitalisation, merchants and marketers all around the world have the privilege to relocate their marketing activities wisely among a lot of different online marketing channels. Those channels can be used exclusively or complementary within their given possibilities (Bormann, 2019, p. 131). The different benefits coming with each channel should not only be bundled, but also cleverly combined in order to profit from their different synergies (Schilling, 2019, p. 92). About 95% of all marketers, being responsible for business-to-business as well as business-to-customer marketing, say that it is crucial to have a multi-channel online marketing strategy in order to generate as much sales or leads as possible. In addition, this is supported by the fact that users are more likely to give away their information or buy a product, if they get in touch with a certain advertisement via every online channel being used frequently (Bormann, 2019, p. 131). As a consequence, alternately to cannibalising each other, the different digital marketing channels cooperate and contribute to a better overall customer communication (Duffy, 2004, p. 359). This leads to the redirection of more valuable customers to the merchant's website (Gregori, Daniele, & Altinay, 2014, p. 196). Having said this, companies should have a well-thought of multi-channel online marketing strategy in order to maximise their profits and reach the customer in every part of the customer journey (Denzin, 2020; Littmann, 2020). As mentioned in *chapter 3.1*, affiliate marketing is one of the oldest online marketing techniques and hence, shall not be missed in the overall online marketing mix (iProspect, 2020). Besides its own function of generating additional revenue for companies, it can contribute positively to the results of the other marketing channels as well. "The probability of a conversion increases, for example, if users become aware of a merchant through an affiliate website before conducting an online search" (Olbrich, Schultz, & Bormann, 2019, p. 50).

Furthermore, as mentioned in *chapter 3.3.1*, the different external affiliation links, redirecting to a company's website, contribute positively to the respective ranking on the different search engines. As a consequence, the merchant's approach of search engine optimisation is actively supported (Daniele et al., 2009, p. 347). However, it has to be highlighted that there is also the probability of a negative impact of affiliate marketing on search engine advertising. This may arise, when the merchant does not pay special attention to the choice of the affiliate partners. Especially so-called pay-per-click affiliates are likely to use the merchants' name or offer in their search advertisements as well as in the corresponding keyword selection. As a consequence, the performance of the merchants' own search engine advertisements could be harmed by increasing click prices (Denzin, 2019, p. 22). In this context, it has to be mentioned that affiliate marketing is not only capable of supporting the other online marketing approaches, but also vice versa. For example, the social media channel has proven to be incremental for raising awareness and interest for a company's products or services. Furthermore, a company's brand perception on social media is said to contribute positively on the overall consumer behaviour and attitude towards a brand, as people are often using social media for inspirational purposes. Consequently, the willingness to click on an affiliation link and converting on a company's website is increasing (Haimson et al., 2015, p. 3809; Olbrich, Schultz, & Bormann, 2019, p. 52).

3.4 AFFILIATE MARKETING AND THE TRAVEL INDUSTRY

The purpose of this chapter is to understand the fundamental actors of the online travel marketing sector and put affiliate marketing into line with this industry. Additionally, the overall importance and integration of affiliate marketing in the online travel marketing mix is outlined.

3.4.1 DIFFERENTIATION OF ONLINE TRAVEL MARKETING ACTORS

Talking about affiliate marketing in the travel industry, it has to be considered that there are three different actors in the game. First of all, there are the large online travel agencies being a very established way of booking travel and tourism services. The main characteristic of online travel agencies like *Booking* or *HRS* is that they are usually internationally operating and having a huge competitive advantage over other travel marketing actors. Online travel agencies are able to provide the users, as well as the suppliers, with a huge amount of different travel options leading to a very broad offer in the online travel sector. If one combines this aspect with the fact that users are able to book via several devices at any time, a certain competitive advantage is given to the online travel agencies. In addition, this online travel marketing actor is perceived to have a leading role in the accommodation marketing sector (Espinet, 2019, pp. 31–32). The next actors in the online travel marketing industry are the so-called metasearch engines. Companies like *Trivago* or *Tripadvisor* are characterised as metasearch engines and support Internet users in understanding and managing the vast amount of travel information being available in the Internet. Hereby, the travel information is usually clustered into different interest groups in order to enhance their usefulness for the users (Vila & González, 2020, p. 174). Moreover, metasearch engines offer hotels and other travel companies the opportunity to generate further sales in an open, often international market and help them to be present to a wide range of potential customers (Willmert & Nayak, 2019, p. 315). Looking at online travel agencies and metasearch engines it has to be mentioned that the lines between these two business models are starting to blur. Metasearch engines have observed the huge success of online travel agencies and started to implement booking functions into their websites. This often results in a lot of metasearch engines transforming into smaller online travel agencies. On the other hand, several online travel agencies have started to implement different search functions into their websites, as they start to understand the usefulness of the metasearch business model (Willmert & Nayak, 2019, p. 324). Last but not least, the third actor in the online travel marketing branch has to be named: the service providers. This includes all travel companies trying to drive their direct bookings with conducting different online marketing activities. Their main objective is to harvest first-hand data and minimise the commission that has to be paid for bookings through online travel agencies (Cendyn, 2017, pp. 2–3). Travel providers offer the possibility for affiliates to participate in their affiliate partner programs, so that the providers' means of advertising can be integrated on the publishers' website and the affiliate promotion process starts. It is likely for travel businesses to work with affiliate networks as an interface, so that the technical requirements are guaranteed, and a valid transaction assignment can take place (Lastminute, 2020). The different affiliate marketing conditions of travel providers are likely to be found on their websites and deliver the most important information regarding essential affiliation aspects, such as integration, commission models, and specific advantages of their affiliate marketing programs (Eurowings, 2020).

3.4.2 THE VALUE OF AFFILIATE MARKETING FOR THE TRAVEL INDUSTRY

Generally speaking, the world wide web and emerging digital distribution possibilities have increased their importance for the travel industry tremendously (Gregori, Daniele, & Altinay, 2014, p. 196). It can be stated that the online sales exceed the offline sales in the travel industry surely and that is why it is of high importance for this sector to implement several traffic-building activities, such as affiliate marketing, into their online marketing strategies. In this context, it has to be mentioned that affiliate marketing activities have shaped the landscape of the online travel industry and its distribution approaches enormously (Gregori, Daniele, & Altinay, 2014, pp. 196–197). Affiliate marketing is seen as a popular and highly effective marketing approach among the travel industry, offering travel companies the possibility to generate further income (Pathak & Saxena, 2019, p. 352; Suchada et al., 2017, p. 132). Having said this, affiliate marketing is perceived to be a major aspect of the strategic online marketing approaches of travel businesses and the travel branch has proven to be one of the most important industries when it comes to the amount of affiliate marketing investments (Middleton et al., 2009, p. 263; Mohamed & Fahmy, 2013, p. 121). Furthermore, especially the cooperation between travel companies and online travel agencies is seen as a popular form of affiliate travel marketing (Septiawan, Nadra, & Astuti, 2018, p. 26). With those strategic alliances, travel companies are able to identify the strengths of their affiliate partners and use them for their own differentiation approaches (Middleton et al., 2009, p. 389). Furthermore, intelligent affiliate marketing partnerships offer smaller travel companies the opportunity to outsource their e-booking systems. By partnering with, for example, an online travel agency, the need for having an integrated e-booking system is eliminated (Mousavi, 2012, p. 35). Besides the general opportunities of affiliate marketing, being further described in *chapter 3.3.1*, the online marketing channel offers travel companies the advantage of using an e-commerce environment that is not associated with further overhead costs. In addition, affiliate marketing helps travel companies to discover potential new markets and increase their overall brand perception (Daniele et al., 2009, p. 347). By having the opportunity to operate on a global affiliate market, travel companies are able to acquire people from various geographical areas in a relatively easy way (Morozan & Enache, 2013, p. 882). Apart from that, studies have shown that trust is one of the most important factors influencing the booking decisions of users in the affiliate process. It has been proven that the trust in the publishers is crucial for the buying decisions of users, whereas only little influence is attributed to the trust in the travel company itself (Suchada et al., 2017, p. 137). That is why trust is evidenced to lead to an increased "consumer loyalty and commitment" (Mohamed & Fahmy, 2013, p. 121). In this context, it has to be emphasised that it could be difficult for travel companies to build trust in an e-commerce environment, as users may still be likely to associate risks and uncertainty with it (Mohamed & Fahmy, 2013, p. 120). Having said this, the cooperation with certain affiliates that are perceived to have a good reputation, indicates that businesses can reach customers they might not have reached otherwise (Srinivas, Priya, & Pinky, 2018, p. 234). As a consequence, the publisher trend in affiliate travel marketing is showing that less affiliates are successful with the business model of paid search and tend to move towards an affiliate business model being associated with the loyalty or reward publisher sector, when coming to work with companies from the travel industry (Daniele et al., 2009, p. 349). This underlines the mentioned importance of wisely chosen affiliate marketing partners in *chapter 3.3.1*. Another important aspect that has to be considered is that affiliate marketing can be seen as an "important source of customer acquisition and a major strategic issue for travel and tourism companies which market their products online" (Daniele et al., 2009, p. 343). As the travel industry is said to be highly competitive, merchants have to act proactively in order to conduct successful affiliate marketing activities and ensure sufficient returns on investment. Due to the high competition in this industry, the affiliate marketing programs have to be designed and constantly updated in a close relationship with the affiliates and possible affiliate networks. It has been proven that only tailor-made affiliate programs can ensure the success of affiliate marketing in the travel industry (Daniele et al, 2009, p. 353).

4 METHODOLOGY

The purpose of this chapter is to give insights into the empirical procedure of the executed research. This refers to the chosen research method, sample selection approach and data analysis technique.

4.1 RESEARCH METHOD

When speaking of empirical research methodologies, three different approaches come into mind: qualitative, quantitative, and mixed research (Lehnen, 2017, p. 95). For the purpose of this research, the qualitative research approach in terms of expert interviews has been selected. The interviews were designed in an open and semi-structured way in order to give the interviewees the possibility to answer the questions freely and generate an open interview atmosphere. Furthermore, the interviews were designed to focus on the related aspects of the two previously defined research questions. The priorly conducted literature research (*chapter 2 et seq.* and *3 et seq.*) has given valuable insights into the relevant topics of business intelligence, affiliate marketing, and travel marketing. Based on these insights, interview guidelines have been developed in order to make sure that every important aspect of the subjects are covered. That is why the interview guidelines consist of two different parts, each being committed to another research question. This implies that the questions of the first part mainly aim at getting insights into the importance of business intelligence on targeting, retargeting, other marketing decisions, efficiency, and possible limitations with regard to its application in affiliate marketing. The second part was designed to show the overall value of affiliate marketing for the travel industry and bring this in line with business intelligence and its impact on the efficiency and competitive advantage of travel businesses. For the purpose of gaining insights into the research topic, seven expert interviews were scheduled, conducted, and recorded with the help of different virtual conference and recording tools. In order to make the interviews as comfortable as possible for the interview partners, the interview guidelines were distributed along with the confirmation of the interview date. This was done in both English and German, so that they could choose their preferred interview language individually. Furthermore, this implied that the interviewees could gain previous insights into the topics and knew what to expect. As a security, the experts were asked to fill out individual interview consent forms before the expert interviews were executed. This ensured that the author was evidently allowed to record the answers given and use them later on for the purpose of this research.

4.2 SAMPLE SELECTION

After the right research method has been chosen, experts for the qualitative research needed to be selected carefully.

Having said this, an expert can be characterised as an individual who is professionally qualified and competent enough to have substantial knowledge about a certain subject (Bogner, Littig, & Menz, 2014, pp. 9–10). In order to guarantee the representativeness of this paper, the experts chosen can be associated to all areas being involved and affected by business intelligence and affiliate marketing in the travel industry. As a consequence, internationally operating affiliate marketing managers, data scientists, merchants, and affiliates from the travel sector examine the topic from different perspectives with the objective to support the research conveyed. Subsequent to the establishment of the important expert characteristics, the author had to get in contact with the perceived industry professionals. Due to the digital character of the research topic and former experiences, the expert acquisition took place via the digital business network *LinkedIn*. First of all, different experts of the industries were contacted via friend requests. After a successful connection had taken place, the experts were contacted with a follow-up message, briefly explaining the purpose of the research and interview design as such. Furthermore, the interview guidelines were attached, in order to give the experts a better overview of what to expect and support an estimation whether they are capable of supporting the research with their reliable expertise. Due to the very open communication on *LinkedIn*, the messages were formulated in a friendly and relaxed manner. It can be said that the business platform proved to be the right medium in order to find qualified experts, as it was easy to contact a large amount of industry professionals in a short period of time. This ensured that this research could be supported with a lot of industry expertise.

4.3 DATA ANALYSIS TECHNIQUE

After all expert interviews had been conducted via virtual conferencing systems, such as *Skype* and *Google Hangouts*, an appropriate data analysis technique needed to be found. In order to obtain superior knowledge from the answers given, the expert interviews were transcribed carefully. Due to the chosen data analysis technique, the virtual conferences were recorded (audio only) with the free *Apple Voice Memos* application in order to prevent any loss of information. The next step, the transcription of the audio sequences, was done both tool-assisted and manually. First of all, the audio files were uploaded into an artificial intelligence based online transcription tool, named *Sonix*. The technology transcribed the expert interviews in their origin language, being either English or German, and gave the author the opportunity to work with the audio file and its corresponding transcription within the online application. In order to ensure that every information has been transcribed correctly and without the loss of valuable information, the author reviewed and corrected eventual transcription and grammar mistakes. After all interviews have been conducted and transcribed thoroughly, the coding of the interview answers and their correlation to the relevant study aspects and research questions has been executed. The author has done this step manually in order to get a better feeling for the answers given. For this purpose, the expert interviews have been exported as PDF-files and important information has been highlighted manually in a PDF reading tool. Last but not least, the valuable interview answers were structured within a table, so that the different correlations of the responses and research aspects could be shown easily. As a consequence, a proper formulation of the discussion chapter (*5 et seq.*) was ensured.

5 THE IMPORTANCE OF BUSINESS INTELLIGENCE IN AFFILIATE MARKETING

The purpose of this chapter is to outline the qualitative research results regarding the research topic of the importance of business intelligence in affiliate marketing. The topic is discussed critically in order to come to a profound conclusion. Furthermore, the importance is subsequently applied to travel marketing as an example industry. The conducted research, as being described in *chapter 4.1*, is based on seven expert interviews, whereas it is ensured that every expert is professionally and closely related to the research topic chosen.

I1: HRS Group, Business Owner formerly Affiliate Marketing Manager

I2: Intercontinental Hotels Group (IHG), Affiliate Specialist

I3: Leading e-commerce business operating various travel portals, Online Marketing Manager Affiliates

I4: German e-commerce business operating various travel websites, Data Analyst

I5: SilverTours GmbH, Team Lead Advertising & Cooperations

I6: reisetopia GmbH, Founder & Manager Partner Cooperations

I7: SaphirSolution, Affiliate Marketing Manager

5.1 TARGETING AND RETARGETING

In order to conduct successful affiliate marketing campaigns, it is crucial to know which customer segments a company needs to approach and, subsequently, if this has been executed properly (I1). Having said this, business intelligence offers marketers a broad range of new possibilities to target specific customer groups that were not possible to target before. The integration of business intelligence ensures that affiliate marketing managers can combine different data sets in order to develop accurate user profiles (I3) and even create defined user personas that are used throughout the whole company (I4). As a consequence, affiliate marketing managers can consider and review customers easily in order to get the most out of the affiliate marketing campaigns conducted (I3). With the usage of data-driven approaches, it is possible to identify different customer niches that may be interesting for the business as such. Affiliate marketing is able to target those customer segments and position the company in smaller environments, where the competitors might not be present. Furthermore, the advanced targeting options, coming along with the integration of business intelligence, offer affiliate marketing managers the possibilities to display their specific means of advertising only to those people, for whom they are actually interesting and relevant (I6). This finding is additionally supported by the respective outcomes of *chapter 2.4*. Having said this, the benefits of being very granular and precise with the different audience selections (I2) are further enhanced with the possibility to develop so-called statistical twins (I3). Those statistical twins enable affiliate marketers to conduct predicted targeting, meaning that through the usage of business intelligence, it is possible to use the data collected and establish target groups being similar to the people who, for example, have bought their products or the ones of the competitors (I5). Even though it might seem very easy for affiliate marketing managers to support their targeting activities with the integration of business intelligence in their decision-making processes, it has to be considered, that it is often quite hard for data analysts to actually transfer the perceived customer definitions and groups into the business intelligence processes. Having said this, it is important to highlight that not all data can be processed or displayed the way it may be needed for the perceived customer segments and affiliation processes. Data analysts have to find new ways to transfer the marketers' targeting needs into the world of business intelligence and build advanced solutions to get the desired results (I1).

Another important aspect that has to be considered is the impact of business intelligence on the retargeting approaches of affiliate marketing managers. Even though some companies might have a different department for this type of marketing (I2), retargeting can still be part of various affiliate marketing activities. The integration of several business intelligence technologies enables marketers to analyse the data sets collected and define different customer segments based on their previous interactions with the respective companies (I3). In addition, business intelligence systems help to apply the information gained in order to reactivate former customers effectively and reward them for their previous interactions with the businesses (I6). For example, marketers are able to answer the question whether a certain user has been a previous customer or prospect (I1), reactivate and reward this user accordingly with the usage of explicit coupon codes being attractive for this sort of customer segment (I3). By using business intelligence as an assistance in different retargeting approaches, affiliate marketing managers are able to easily remind the customer about the merchants' products or services and hence, it has proven to be a very promising field in the affiliation space (I7). These aspects are further supported by the findings of *chapter 2.2.3*, examining the needs-driven decision-making approach that refers to finding solutions to certain business questions with the assistance of business intelligence technologies. Another very auspicious facet of the usage of business intelligence for affiliate retargeting purposes might be the classification of customers due to their loyalty statuses. Business intelligence is able to determine different loyalty ratings which are able to help affiliate marketing managers to conduct promising retargeting activities and reactivate, for example, those customers who have not interacted with the specific company in a while (I2). Having said this, data-based retargeting activities can help marketers to increase their affiliate advertising pressure and, consequently, result in higher website traffic figures. A good example for this is that if the marketer has been able to acquire a new website visitor through affiliation activities and this specific customer does not convert and bounces instead, affiliate retargeting can help to re-address this customer instantly. The consequently enhanced affiliate advertising pressure may eventually convert the prospect into a promising customer (15). However, it has to be emphasised that the success of retargeting campaigns in the field of affiliate marketing does not rely on the data insights gained solely. It has been proven that different external factors, such as an ongoing crisis, can have a huge impact on the overall buying behaviour of customers and hence, should not be neglected (17).

5.2 GENERAL MARKETING DECISION PROCESS

After considering the specific value of business intelligence technologies for the targeting and retargeting approaches in affiliate marketing, it is of high importance to highlight its impact on further marketing decision processes. Generally speaking, it can be examined that the more data one has, the better decision-making can take place within the company (11). Due to the fact, that digital marketing is getting more and more complex, customers are likely to be harder to reach, and the overall customer demands rise drastically, business intelligence technologies are needed to get a clear overview on what is actually possible and how companies can manage to adapt to the ever-evolving business environments (14).

Having said this, before basing affiliate marketing decisions on the business intelligence insights gained, it has to be determined which data sets are actually valuable for a company and supporting the different affiliate marketing actions. First and foremost, it is crucial to observe the classical affiliate marketing key performance indicators in order to have a base of hard figures to support further marketing decisions (13). Hereby, it has to be regarded, that depending on the underlying campaign objective, the weighting of the different key performance indicators may differ (11). The particular key performance indicators have to be considered per affiliate and campaign separately and mostly include the traffic generated, conversion rate, return on ad spent (15), and click-through-rate achieved, means of advertising and placements used, as well as the customer segment chosen and the specific devolution of the customer journey (I1). As stated in *chapter 2.2.2*, those respective key performance indicators can easily be portrayed by basic business intelligence tools. Furthermore, based on those performance figures, a solid cost-benefit analysis can be conducted, showing the affiliate marketers the profitability of the different campaigns (I4). Having said this, with the determination of valuable data sets, better affiliate marketing decisions can be made (I3). For example, affiliate marketing managers are able to verify a publisher's quality before even starting the partnership. With the usage of different forecasts, being generated by business intelligence technologies, it is possible to predict the success or failures of different publishers and affiliate marketing campaigns (I5). Furthermore, it is crucial to examine the performance and attractiveness of an affiliate in order to be able to select only the affiliates partners that are specifically fitting the purpose of the affiliate marketing campaign. Historical data can then be utilised for evaluating the performance of potential and already onboarded affiliates carefully. As a consequence, the merchant is able to adjust the different contract conditions correspondently. This supports the fac, that the future partnership with an affiliate is decisively subject to its historical performance (I7). This relevant facet can be underlined by the findings of *chapter 2.4.* and *chapter 2.3.1*, showing the incremental importance of business intelligence for the prediction of future scenarios. Additionally, the integration of business intelligence in various decision processes helps merchants to determine precisely which publishers are actually relevant in order to get the most return on investment with the different affiliate marketing campaigns (I6). In this context, the affiliate marketing managers always have to consider the different additional marketing actions that the affiliate partners may have conducted in order to drive their own performance. It is very likely that affiliate partners try to increase their performance by the execution of additional advertisements in, for example, their newsletters. This has to be taken into consideration when evaluating the performances of the different affiliates as such. In addition, business intelligence cannot only help to identify attractive affiliates on an individual basis, but also helps to generate valuable insights which publisher segment has proven to be the most promising for a company's affiliate marketing activities (I7). Furthermore, these business intelligence insights can assist to assess the different utilisations and placements of different means of advertising and show which one has proven to be more efficient (I3). Having said this, merchants are able to test different sets of means of advertising and the corresponding data harvested can give valuable insights in which, for example, banner design works best (I7). Based on this evaluation, affiliate marketing managers can optimise their means of advertising and make profound marketing decisions (I5). Another decision, that can be supported by the usage of business intelligence technologies, is the integration of data-based coupon codes. It is possible to adjust coupon incentives to the different target groups selected (I3) and hence, better leverage the special marketing offers being displayed (I2). In addition to its usage before and during the execution of affiliate marketing campaigns, business intelligence evidently helps marketers to assess the historical data of previous campaigns in order to draw valuable comparisons and evaluate the performance of each campaign individually. With this approach, affiliate marketers are able to observe which affiliate partners have performed best and redirected the more valuable users (I5). This performance evaluation can be utilised later on for the data-based decision-making processes of future affiliate marketing campaigns (I1). Having considered all these aspects, affiliate marketing managers are able to build their respective marketing decisions based on the forecasts being generated by business intelligence and a certain argumentation base is given. Only with the solid marketing decision justification, evolving from the different data technologies, it is manageable for affiliate marketers to create trust in the actions suggested and raise the money being necessary to conduct these activities (I5). This statement is additionally backed up with the overall importance of data-driven decision-making, being examined in *chapter 2.2.3*. Furthermore, in the case of badly performing affiliate marketing campaigns, the different data insights can help companies to identify the source of failures (for example, caused by the affiliate, means of advertising, coupon code, or product of the merchant) and adjust the campaigns accordingly in order to increase the success (I7).

5.3 EFFICIENCY AND MUST-DOS OF BUSINESS INTELLIGENCE INTEGRATION

First of all, it has to be mentioned that business intelligence is inevitable for the successful implementation of affiliate marketing campaigns nowadays (I3). Moreover, affiliate marketing managers are able to use business intelligence technologies to base their strategies on it and get the most out of every affiliate marketing action. Additionally, they are able to work very granularly and improve the campaigns' performance on a continuous basis (I2). Without the usage of data-driven technologies, it is extremely difficult for affiliate marketers to evaluate a campaigns' performance accurately and see which different methods perform the best (I5). Due to the fact that business intelligence technologies deliver data insights in real-time (I6), it is easy for affiliate managers to see if something is wrong with an affiliate marketing campaign and hence, they can react immediately in order to stabilise its performance (I4). Having said this, the integration of business intelligence increases efficiency throughout the whole company, as everyone working with it uses the same data base. This helps significantly to improve performance, as a common ground and language is given and, consequently, structure and facilitation of the daily business activities can be achieved (I4). These findings are backed up by the results of *chapter 2.4*. In addition to this aspect, business intelligence encourages clever investments in affiliate marketing, as it prevents to partner with inefficient publishers. Furthermore, it assists to identify early which market development funds will bring promising results in the affiliation industry. As a consequence, an efficient cost structure can be ensured (I5). Having said this, the in *chapter 5.1* described targeting options through the integration of business intelligence allow to set-up efficient affiliate marketing campaigns. An adequate performance is assured which results in avoiding having to use special coupon codes in order to grab the customers' attention. The usage of coupon incentives in affiliate marketing always leads to higher cost figures and thus, is said to be hindering campaigns to be as efficient as possible (I2).

However, the previously mentioned increase in efficiency through the utilisation of business intelligence can only be assured, if several must-dos are executed successfully. First of all, it is of high importance that everyone being involved in the business intelligence processes has some sort of a common ground. A solid basic understanding of business intelligence is needed in order to guarantee an efficiency improvement. Furthermore, this also implies that the different definitions (e.g., of a customer or a sale) within the organisation are clearly communicated, in order to ensure a common operating base (I4). Furthermore, this shows how important a common knowledge base is, as outlined in *chapter 2.5*, to assure the success of business intelligence systems. This aspect is highly connected with the second must-do, the decent communication between all parties being involved. It is crucial that the affiliate marketing and business intelligence departments are communicating proactively with one another in order to ensure an accurate information transfer. Only with this approach, the different benefits of business intelligence can be understood, and it is easier to get the most out of the technologies used (I3). Having said this, the affiliate marketing department has to make sure that they know exactly what they want to extract from the data harvested, as otherwise it may be very hard for the data analysts to assure the perceived outcomes. As it is likely for affiliate marketers to not understand the full capabilities and processes of business intelligence, it is a must-do that they are open to consultancy from the data analysts' side, as they are likely to know best whether an affiliate marketing request can be realised or not (I4). Another must-do would be, that it is of high importance to have data sovereignty and execute the business intelligence processes internally, as much as possible (I1). Efficiency can only be guaranteed, if one is familiar with the own data and knows the exact opportunities coming along with it (I4). The business intelligence department has to have the data under full control (I6) and needs to know exactly how to analyse and visualise the insights properly (I3). It is tremendously important that everyone being involved in the business intelligence processes knows particularly how to handle the business intelligence outcomes. Having said this, the best data insights will not increase affiliate marketing's efficiency, if the parties involved are not able to apply it correctly (I1). The next must-do is that companies have to constantly be up-to-date and need to continually adapt to new innovations arising in the field of business intelligence (I5). Moreover, the processes have to evolve steadily in order to be able to get the most out of the data harvested (I3). This must-do is further supported by the related findings of *chapter 2.1*. As business intelligence is said to be the point of intersection of every online marketing channel (I4), another must-do is that marketers do not consider affiliate marketing as an isolated online marketing channel. It is advised to have a look at all business intelligence insights generated, in order to be able to recreate and analyse the whole customer journey and see exactly, which role affiliate marketing is tending to play for the different touch points (I1). The last must-do that has to be mentioned, is the accurate implementation of data tracking (I6). Even though a lot of affiliate networks are taking the tracking process off the merchants, it is of high importance to implement a separate affiliate tracking approach in order to double-validate the data. Tracking is an important part of the merchant-publisher relationship, as it is often used as the base of remuneration and trust between the parties (I1). This specific must-do highlights the high importance of a proper affiliate marketing tracking implementation, being outlined in *chapter 3.2.4*.

5.4 LIMITATIONS OF BUSINESS INTELLIGENCE APPLICATION

In order to highlight the topic of business intelligence critically, several limitations have to be examined. Moreover, the restrictions of the application of business intelligence can be categorised into legal, technical and entrepreneurial limitations.

The legal limitations are mainly dealing with different laws that have been put into place during the last years. Those laws are restricting the companies in their ability to collect data from customers and are perceived to be ever-evolving. As a consequence, businesses are forced to having to reinvent the ways they work with data and business intelligence in order to act legally correct. Having said this, it is often the case that historical data cannot be used anymore, as several laws prohibit the utilisation of data being collected in a former, different kind (I2). Especially in Europe, the GDPR compliances hinder companies from collecting valuable customer data, as, for example, cookies are not allowed to be set without the explicit consent of the user (I1). Limitations in the cookie tracking process imply, among others, that the users have to actively agree to being tracked and analysed (I3), leading to the loss of a lot of valuable customer data. These findings are supported by the ones being previously outlined in *chapter 3.2.4*, showing that the legal limitations of business intelligence are something affiliate marketers have to face in their daily operations. Additionally, it can be said that there is a constant battle between the granular possibilities of business intelligence and the corresponding different legal restrictions being put in place (I2). Coming to the technical limitations of business intelligence systems, it has to be regarded that there is a definite barrier in what companies are actually able to collect from their customers. Furthermore, as a merchant, it is not possible to access the data from the publisher site (I1) and vice versa. In addition, it is not possible for any affiliate marketing actor to get an overview of the data concerning the whole market (I6) and, especially, the competitors. Spying out of data is not possible and, as a consequence, the characteristics of the competitor's customers are always subject to speculation (I3). Another technical limitation is that business intelligence may not be able to deliver every insight needed. Having said this, not every affiliate marketing need can be satisfied with the usage of business intelligence technologies, as sometimes different data sets simply cannot be combined (I4). Furthermore, the technologies can only work with data being available and are not able to analyse potential external influences that, for example, motivated the user to convert. Hence, it is not possible to determine if affiliate marketing is actually responsible for a certain conversion or if the user would have converted without affiliate marketing, as well. Additionally, the technologies cannot identify exactly, if affiliate marketing was the critical factor of the customer journey that initiated the sale, as they are not able to have a look into the customers' mind (I5). Last but not least, the entrepreneurial limitations have to be considered. Depending on the business model chosen, both, publishers and merchants, are restricted in the data they are able to collect. One example for this limitation would be that not every website is able to collect very detailed customer data, as the specific business model does not imply that customers have to register on the website. As a consequence, business intelligence is stretched to its limits and cannot develop granular customer personas and segments (I6). Another limitation is that affiliate partners are not on the same technological levels and thus, have a hard time implementing the insights of the other parties. This leads to an overall reduction in data usability among the affiliate marketing actors (I2). Having said this, not only the transfer of data between the different affiliate marketing actors shows limitations of business intelligence. The general information transfer within the companies as such is often limited by different organisational rules or entities and hence, business intelligence cannot unlock its full potential (I3). This finding is further supported by the respective aspects being mentioned in *chapter 2.3.3*.

5.5 INTERIM CONCLUSION

The aspects discussed in *chapter 5.1 et seq.* portray the general importance of business intelligence technologies on the digital marketing channel affiliate marketing. In this context, the research question being correlated with this part – *R1: To what extend does business intelligence help to make relevant affiliate marketing decisions?* – has to be regarded. The examined findings evidently demonstrate that business intelligence plays a crucial role in all relevant marketing decisions being associated with affiliate marketing. Data-based decision-making, adapted from predefined and individual key performance indicators, helps affiliate marketers to develop profound marketing strategies and backup their main affiliate marketing decisions such as targeting, retargeting, means of advertising, partner selection, and overall daily performance adjustments. However, the topic has to be examined critically, as the usage of business intelligence in the marketing decision process can be subject to legal, technological, and organisational limitations. As a consequence, the answer to the research question is that business intelligence definitely helps affiliate marketers to make encompassing marketing decisions, but only when the different limitations of usage are taken into consideration. In order to overcome a lot of those obstacles, it is highly important for affiliate marketers to back up their processes with the highlighted must-dos for a proper business intelligence integration. This assists companies in the reduction of any risks and biases that may occur in the data-based marketing decision process and, therefore, helps to ensure a good affiliate marketing performance.

5.6 TRAVEL MARKETING

The objective of this chapter is to put the importance of business intelligence and affiliate marketing into relation with the travel industry.

5.7 GENERAL VALUE OF AFFILIATE MARKETING FOR THE TRAVEL INDUSTRY

Speaking of the overall value of affiliate marketing for the travel industry, it has to be mentioned that its success in this branch is inevitable (I3). The main reason for that is that it is perceived as a supplementary channel within the online travel marketing mix, whose intention of usage is to generate additional sales to the already existing daily business. Having said this, the online marketing channel has proven to be very cost-efficient, so that there is no financial risk coming with it (I1). As a consequence, travel companies are able to reach an extremely low cost of sale with the implementation of affiliate marketing (I2). These findings fit to the previously analysed opportunities of affiliate marketing for companies, being examined in *chapter 3.3.1*.

However, the success and opportunities of affiliate marketing are always connected to different determinants. First and foremost, it has to be mentioned that affiliate marketing should not be perceived as an isolated digital marketing approach, as it has proven to be dependent on the success of other online marketing activities. In this context, it is crucial for travel companies to have a well-developed online marketing mix in order to benefit from different synergies emerging. Furthermore, it is tremendously important for travel businesses to have a very appealing and well-developed website, ideally being conversion-optimised, so that the users can easily convert, and affiliate marketing campaign objectives can be accomplished (I7). This again highlights the importance of a proper integration of affiliate marketing into the overall online marketing mix, being emphasised in *chapter 3.3.2*. Another determinant would be that depending on the business model, the competition, and customer behaviour, affiliate marketing is able to help travel companies to generate further sales or leads and thus, enhance their overall revenue figures. As the travel industry and its related products or services are highly emotional and need to fulfil certain customer needs, affiliate marketing can help the businesses to convince respective customers with being present on a wide range of travel relevant partner websites. These partners are for example important travel blogs or magazines. Since the booking of, for instance, a vacation is usually not perceived as an impulsive purchase (I5) and the overall competition in the travel online market is extremely vigorous (I3), travel companies have to invest a lot into their marketing activities in order to win the customer's favour. Having said this, businesses have to fight for every client, as the online travel market can be characterised as an oligopoly (I5). Especially for hotel brands, it is extremely difficult to keep pace with large travel businesses like online travel agencies, as these are able to offer competitive prices for nearly every hotel one can think of and, therefore, it is relatively demanding for individual hotel brands to generate direct bookings (I2). This aspect is further backed up with the general market power perception of online travel agencies, being emphasised in *chapter 3.4.1*. However, this circumstance can be diminished by strategic partnerships with the right affiliates in the travel industry. It is crucial for travel companies to choose the right partners to work with in order to get the most out of the affiliate marketing activities and align those with the predefined campaign objectives. However, it is observed to be quite difficult to find those strategic partners, as the amount of premium affiliate partners is limited within the travel industry. Only a few large affiliate partners have proven to be really profitable and these publishers are definitely aware of their great market positions. As a consequence, a lot of the high-quality partners demand immense market development funds for special placements on their websites. That is why it is often a huge challenge for travel companies to identify which partners are actually worth working with and, more importantly, which partners are worth investing in (I3). However, if travel businesses are able to connect with great travel blogs and large couponing affiliates, those partnerships can be extremely profitable. As a matter of fact, users are tending to inform themselves about travel destinations and possibilities in different travel blogs and magazines (I5). Hereby, affiliate marketing comes into play. It offers travel companies the possibility to integrate their means of advertising nearly invisibly in those relevant travel blogs and magazines, so that the users are often not even realising that a certain promotion is being executed (I3). Especially in the travel industry, affiliate marketing is extremely interesting, as it gives companies of different travel niches the opportunity to partner up with each other and create complementary products. Affiliate partnerships of, for example, airlines and accommodation providers, have shown that affiliate marketing has a huge potential in this industry (I1). This important facet can be further supported by the findings being examined in *chapter 3.4.2*. Another aspect that has to be considered in the field of affiliate travel marketing is the subject of profit margins and related usage of coupon incentives. Generally speaking, the profit margins are very little in this industry and hence, coupon codes have to be played very targeted and with a lot of deliberation (I5). Due to its very transparent cost structure, affiliate marketing can help travel businesses to leverage their marketing costs and, for example, marketers only have to pay the affiliates a certain commission fee that is realisable within their individual profit margin (I6). This additionally emphasises the benefit of the underlying concept of a performance-based marketing approach, being further examined in *chapter 3.3.1*. As mentioned before, the online travel industry is subject to a lot of competition. Having said this, the logical consequence is that businesses have to attract customers with compelling offers, often resulting in special coupon incentives in the affiliate marketing field (I2). Customers, being acquired through affiliate travel marketing actions, are perceived to be very price sensitive and, therefore, coupon incentives are often helpful and necessary to push them indirectly into the direction of a merchant's travel website (I3). However, it has to be taken into account that this customer behaviour may lead to a certain problem arising in affiliate travel marketing. Customers being active on publisher websites, such as coupon or cashback affiliates, are very likely to look for the best deals or cashbacks possible. Furthermore, the affiliate travel marketing environment has proven to attract more leisure than business guests. Business bookings are usually generated without any price comparisons, but on the other hand, leisure guests (such as families) tend to compare different prices and are mainly active on the relevant affiliate travel websites (I2). As a consequence, affiliate marketing is usually not able to deliver long-term customers to the travel businesses, as the affiliate customers acquired are perceived to be loyal to the price instead of the travel brand as such (I1).

5.7.1 BUSINESS INTELLIGENCE IN AFFILIATE TRAVEL MARKETING

As mentioned in *chapter 5.3*, the integration of business intelligence technologies increases the overall efficiency of affiliate marketing campaigns evidently and helps marketers to get the best out of this digital marketing channel. Nevertheless, for answering the research question – *R2: Does business intelligence improve the efficiency of affiliate marketing activities in online travel marketing?* – correctly, the subsequent has to be taken into consideration:

Especially in the field of travel marketing, business intelligence is extremely relevant for executing successful affiliate marketing campaigns. Besides the classical affiliate marketing key performance indicators, being further described in *chapter 5.3*, business intelligence can help travel companies to get valuable insights into special customer segments being highly relevant for this industry. For example, it is possible to analyse the time difference between the first click on the mean of advertising and the actual booking of a travel product or service (I1). Another aspect would be that companies can identify exactly how long it has been since a customer has booked his last stay or flight and hence, individual retargeting through affiliate travel marketing activities can be conducted. Furthermore, the successful implementation of business intelligence can help travel businesses to understand their customers' needs during a stay on a whole new level. The data being collected during a stay in, for example, a special hotel, can help to target customers with tailored offers and assists to get the most out of the affiliate marketing campaigns. In addition, travel companies can analyse patterns of the length of stays in accommodations and are able to get important insights on the actual value of different customer segments. Consequently, it is possible to display the right offer to the right clients and be more efficient in the affiliate travel marketing activities conducted (I2). As the travel industry is subject to different seasonal aspects, such as summer or winter business, it is important to use business intelligence in order to draw different comparisons within the affiliate marketing field. Business intelligence technologies help travel organisations to compare the data harvested on a weekly, monthly, and yearly basis, which offers the benefit of having a great overview over the performance during the different seasons. Hence, affiliate marketing managers are able to operate more efficiently (I5). These findings highlight the importance of data-driven decision-making for enhancing a company's efficiency, being examined in *chapter 2.2.3*. Having said this, it is of high importance to evaluate the affiliate travel marketing performance based on a specific time period, as affiliate campaigns are likely to need a few weeks for launching properly (I7). Especially in affiliate travel marketing, it is tremendously important to always be up-to-date and able to optimise campaigns immediately. Consequently, another important aspect is the possibility of analysing data concerning the traffic and cancelation ratio. It might be the case that some affiliates generate a lot of traffic through the redirection to the travel company's website, but after a while, a lot of those alleged customers cancel their bookings. This leads to a bad result in the overall figures and can be monitored and prevented through the usage of business intelligence technologies (I5). As a consequence, companies can identify insufficient affiliates and restrain inefficient affiliate travel marketing partnerships. In order to prevent that the merchants pay affiliates for bookings that have been cancelled, it is crucial to use inventory data for identifying possible cancellations and report them immediately to the affiliate marketing system after a specific reversal time has passed (I7). The importance of business intelligence insights for real-time decision-making is further underlined by the findings of *chapter 2.1.* and *chapter 2.2.1.* Having said this, the usage of business intelligence for affiliate marketing purposes in the travel industry increases its efficiency tremendously (I2). In addition to the in *chapter 5.3* examined overall efficiency increase in affiliate marketing through the utilisation of business intelligence, several efficiency aspects apply especially to the field of travel marketing. With an accurate integration and usage, it is possible to understand travel customers better and target them very granularly. Furthermore, it helps to continuously monitor and improve the performance of ongoing affiliate travel marketing campaigns (I2). Travel campaigns can be conducted more precisely (I3) and business intelligence helps to determine which affiliate travel campaign performs best or worse in order to compensate one with another. The aspect of having historical data retrievable at any time helps to keep an eye on every important affiliate marketing aspect and hence, travel companies know exactly when they need to adjust something (I5). As a consequence, business intelligence obtains that affiliate marketers can bring their affiliate travel programs on a whole new level of efficiency (I2). These findings are supported by the overall business intelligence benefits for companies, being further emphasised in *chapter 2.4*. Furthermore, affiliate marketers are able to make efficient data-based decisions, resulting in a stabilised cost allocation that is protecting the little travel profit margin. Furthermore, a precise coupon code playout can be guaranteed, when needed (I3).

Having said this, the generated insights and the increase of the affiliate marketing efficiency in travel marketing, help travel companies to gain a significant competitive advantage. Here, the theory of Porter and Millar, concerning the gain of competitive advantage through information (as stated in *chapter 2.3.1*), applies. The usage of business intelligence as a sustainable concept throughout the whole organisation (I4) assists travel companies with benefitting from the data collected and ensures a very good understanding of existing and potential customers. Due to this gain of knowledge, affiliate travel marketing campaigns can be conducted more efficiently (I3) and the marketers are able to identify easily the worth of each customer being acquired. In addition, travel companies can evaluate how much marketing budget should be used in affiliate marketing in the long-term, in order to stabilise a good cost allocation (I4). Business intelligence insights make it possible for affiliate marketing managers to form evidenced affiliate marketing decisions, resulting in a potentially lower cost structure (I5). This may be, for example, the intelligent investment into certain traffic-building methods, so that a company is able to outperform the others in terms of the cost of sale (I6). Having said this, these findings are supported by the respective outcomes of *chapter 2.1*. Furthermore, the efficient and data-based exploitation of affiliate marketing budget can lead to a higher advertising pressure and presence on all potential customer touchpoints (I7), resulting in an overall improvement of the company's brand awareness. As a consequence, this improvement helps travel companies to increase their overall market power (I5). This aspect is further bolstered by the respective findings of *chapter 3.4.2*. Furthermore, with the efficient decision-making due to a successful business intelligence integration, travel companies are able to scale their affiliate marketing activities and generate, for example, more direct bookings than their specific competitors (I6). Generally speaking, a competitive advantage through business intelligence can be achieved whenever the data harvested and analysed is applied correctly and the other competitors are likely to use business intelligence technologies in another way or not at all (I3).

Summing up the findings of *chapter 5.3* and *chapter 5.6.2*, the research question – *R2: Does business intelligence improve the efficiency of affiliate marketing activities in online travel marketing?* – can be answered as follows: business intelligence has proven to have a huge impact on the efficiency level of travel companies. This applies especially, when it comes to the execution of affiliate marketing in the online travel marketing mix. The findings have shown that business intelligence leads to a smarter decision-making in terms of audience selections, smart investments and real-time campaign optimisation. Consequently, this causes a huge improvement of the performance of respective affiliate marketing campaigns. Having said this, the integration of business intelligence technologies enables a strong understanding of existing and future customers that helps to execute affiliate marketing campaigns extremely efficiently. Furthermore, it is possible to create tailored offers for specific target groups and stabilise the overall affiliate marketing cost allocation, so that the little profit margin of travel products and services can be protected. In addition, this efficiency improvement can further lead to the gain of market power and sustainable competitive advantage. However, an improvement in affiliate marketing efficiency and the resulting possible competitive advantage can only be ensured, if business intelligence is used properly and travel companies are able to outperform their competitors successfully.

6 CONCLUSION

To conclude the findings of this study, one can clearly say that it has proven the major importance of a proper business intelligence integration into the affiliate marketing activities conducted in the travel industry. The usage of different business intelligence technologies does not only support the general decision-making processes in affiliate marketing but does also lead to an improvement of the overall efficiency of the affiliate travel marketing campaigns being executed. Business intelligence, as a sustainable and holistic approach, has proven to be inevitable for making profound decisions in every step of the affiliation process. This does not only contain obvious customer-related decisions, such as the targeting of affiliate marketing campaigns, but starts with the right publisher selection, based on historical data, and ends with the detailed report of certain key performance indicators of a conducted affiliate marketing campaign. Having said this, this approach can be perceived as the never-ending circle of business intelligence application in affiliate marketing, as the performance reports can always function as the new base for future decision-making processes. The different insights gained through business intelligence help affiliate marketers to make real-time and future decisions in order to get the most out of their affiliate marketing activities. Even though the application of business intelligence is somehow stretched to its limits, its overall positive impact is inevitable. Having said this, the implementation and usage of business intelligence in the affiliate marketing process can only benefit companies, if certain must-dos are taken into consideration. It is indispensable for companies to build a common ground of knowledge and acceptance regarding the business intelligence technologies in order to be able to apply it correctly. This foundation has to be realised thoroughly through the whole organisation, from top-level to lower-level managers and employees, in order to guarantee data-driven success. Furthermore, it is crucial that the affiliate marketing and business intelligence departments communicate actively and openly with each other, so that the workflow is made as easy as possible for both sides. As a consequence, misinterpretations of the data analysed can be prevented. However, especially the travel industry is benefitting from the utilisation of business intelligence in affiliate marketing. As this branch is considered to be a highly competitive market, business intelligence insights help the companies to better structure their affiliate marketing activities and, consequently, make the right decisions for this online marketing channel. By striking up well-thought of strategic affiliate partnerships with other travel companies, complementary products can be found and synergies between different travel businesses evolve. This helps the travel organisations to not only increase their overall sales figures, but also assists with the enhancement of their brand perception and awareness by building up a high reach. With those synergies, affiliate travel marketing offers travel companies a whole new world of bringing their products and services to the market. Furthermore, the integration of business intelligence technologies helps travel companies to increase their level of efficiency in this online marketing channel significantly. Having said this, low cost structures, intelligent investments, and very granular targeting methods emerge out of the successful usage of business intelligence in affiliate travel marketing. As the profit margins are relatively low in the travel industry, business intelligence technologies help companies to invest rationally and stabilise a good cost-benefit calculation. In this context, the usage of inefficient coupon incentives and investments in non-promising affiliate placements are prevented by the extraction of valuable customer and publisher information. As a consequence, travel companies are able to display the right affiliate marketing means of advertising to the right target group and obtain highly efficient campaign results. Furthermore, the data insights given offer the benefit of being able to react and adjust affiliate travel marketing campaigns in real-time in order to prevent potential efficiency losses.

Having said this, the considered aspects do not only lead to an improved efficiency level but also assist travel companies with gaining a competitive advantage. The travel industry is perceived to be a highly competitive market in which the usage of business intelligence systems can help to outperform competitors and protect current market positions while simultaneously shaping the future. However, it has to be mentioned that it is only possible for travel businesses to outperform their competitors as long as they use business intelligence systems sufficiently and their respective competitors are using it in a different way or not at all.

7 RECOMMENDATIONS

The purpose of this chapter is to give practical recommendations and recommendations for future research.

7.1 PRACTICAL RECOMMENDATIONS

After having examined the topic of this research carefully, the author gives practical recommendations for the people working with business intelligence in affiliate marketing within the travel industry. These recommendations suggest the following:

— The general acceptance of business intelligence technologies has to be guaranteed throughout the company.
— A common ground and basic knowledge regarding business intelligence has to be assured among all parties being involved.
— The proactive and open communication between the business intelligence and affiliate marketing departments is inevitable.
— Publishers and affiliate marketing campaign performances have to be carefully monitored and evaluated in order to ensure a stable and high return on investment.
— Tracking technologies have to be installed accurately, so that a foundation of trust is given among the merchant and the affiliate.
— Strategic affiliate partnerships have to be executed in order to generate complementary travel products and increase the market power.
— The seasonality within the travel industry has to be taken into consideration when it comes to the evaluation of the affiliate travel marketing performance.
— Business intelligence has to be deployed in affiliate marketing in order to stabilise the little profit margin in the travel industry and

prevent a decrease in efficiency through the deployment of unintelligent travel coupon incentives.
— Business intelligence has to be deployed in order to ensure efficiency in affiliate marketing and realise a sustainable competitive advantage.
— Competitive advantage can only be achieved and protected, if travel companies constantly adapt to the ever-evolving business environments and ensure a consistent customer understanding.

7.2 Recommendations for Future Research

The recommendations for future research imply that further research should be done in the field of the online travel industry, as this seems to be a huge part of the current digital economy. Talking about affiliate marketing in general, it would be advisable to conduct research from the publisher and consumer perspective. Unfortunately, the main focus of existing research in this field relies on the perspective of the merchant solely. Further research should be done in the fields of affiliate marketing and business intelligence, as both subjects are relatively old and established and it would be interesting to examine the subjects' changes from their first steps to the current status quo.

Furthermore, it would be very interesting to research more in the field of possible affiliate marketing partnerships within the travel industry, as the different correlations between online travel agencies, travel providers, and meta-search engines seem extremely relevant and promising. Sticking to the travel industry, it would be worthwhile to examine the further impact of business intelligence on other digital marketing channels (such as SEA, display or social media advertising) or different travel offer strategies. This would help to get a broader overview of the general value of business intelligence for the travel marketing industry, so that further best practices could be developed.

8 LIMITATIONS OF STUDY

Concerning the conducted study, the author determines some limitations that may have restrained the research conducted. Those limitations might have prevented the examination of the research topic within a greater framework. It was hard to find proper former research in the field of travel marketing, which resulted in the subject being narrowed down to its essentials. Moreover, the ongoing circumstances due to the COVID-19 virus have led to a crash within the travel industry. This made it difficult for the author to find experts in said industry, as their priorities and minds are dealing with the outcomes of the crisis.

Nevertheless, the assumed bias and the consequences of the COVID-19 crisis will not lead to the outcomes of this study being less relevant or adaptable for future research and practical applications within the field of the research topic.

9 REFERENCE LIST

Abas, Z. A., Rahman, A. F. N. A., Pramudya, G., Wee, S. Y., Kasmin, F., Yusof, N., Yunos, N. M, and Abidin, Z. Z. (2020). Analytics: a review of current trends, future application and challenges. *COMPUSOFT: An International Journal of Advanced Computer Technology*, 9(1), 3560–3565. Retrieved 16/04/2020, from https://search.proquest.com/openview/2b86215046f231280fa4352262e3e70a/1?cbl=2032622&pq-origsite=gscholar.

Alnoukari, M. and Hanano, A. (2017). Integration of business intelligence with corporate strategic management. *Journal of Intelligence Studies in Business*, 7(2), 5–16. DOI: 10.37380/jisib.v7i2.235.

Amarasekara, B. (2016). *Analysis, Design and Simulation of Fraud and Vulnerability Management in Affiliate Marketing.* DOI: 10.13140/RG.2.2.28121.21603.

Amarasekara, B. and Mathrani, A. (2016). *Controlling risks and fraud in affiliate marketing: a simulation and testing environment.* DOI: 10.1109/PST.2016.7906986.

Arefin, S., Hoque, R., and Bao, Y. (2015). The Impact on Business Intelligence on Organization's Effectiveness: An Empirical Study. *Journal of Systems and Information Technology*, 17 (3), 263–285. DOI: 10.1108/JSIT-09-2014-0067.

Aufaure, M., Chiky, R., Curé, O., Khrouf, H., and Kepeklian, G. (2015). From Business Intelligence to semantic data stream management. *Future Generation Computer Systems*, 63(C), 100–107. DOI: 10.1016/j.future.2015.11.015.

Bahga, A. and Madisetti, V. (2019). *Big Data Science & Analytics. A Hands-On Approach.* Self-Published.

Bala, M. and Verma, D. (2018). A Critical Review of Digital Marketing. *International Journal of Management, IT & Engineering*, 8(10), 321–339. Retrieved 05/04/2020, from https://www.researchgate.net/publication/328253026_A_Critical_Review_of_Digital_Marketing.

Balakrishnan, S. and Rahul, R. (2018). Big Data in Business Intelligence. *CSI Communications*, 21–23. Retrieved 13/03/2020, from https://www.researchgate.net/profile/Balakrishnan_S2/publication/328808426_Big_Data_in_Business_Intelligence/links/5be437d792851c6b27afcd05/Big-Data-in-Business-Intelligence.pdf.

Reference list

Bangari, M., Panwar, D., and Thakur, S. K. (2019). Determinants of Profitable Niche of Affiliate Marketing in Amazon.Com. *Pacific Business Review International*, 11 (12), 130–133. Retrieved 23/03/2020, from https://www.researchgate.net/publication/336230890_Determinants_of_Profitable_Niche_of_Affiliate_Marketing_in_AmazonCom.

Bogner, A., Littig, B., and Menz, W. (2014). *Interviews mit Experten. Eine praxisorientierte Einführung [Interviews with experts. A practice-oriented introduction]*. Springer. DOI: 10.1007/978-3-531-19416-5.

Bormann, P.M. (2019). *Affiliate Marketing. Steuerung des Klickpfads im Rahmen einer Mehrkanalstrategie [Affiliate marketing. Governance of the click funnel of a multichannel strategy]*. Springer Gabler. DOI: 10.1007/978-3-658-25585-5.

Brito, S. M., Briegas, J. J. M., and Iglesias, A. I. S. (2019). Creativity for business intelligence. *International Journal of Developmental and Educational Psychology*, 1(1), 155–164. DOI: 10.17060/ijodaep.2019.n1.v1.1401.

Cambridge University Press (2020). *Maturity*. Retrieved 13/03/2020, from https://dictionary.cambridge.org/de/worterbuch/englisch/maturity.

Cendyn, (2017). *How to combat OTAs & drive direct hotel bookings*. Retrieved 10/04/2020, from https://www.edhotels.com/wp-content/uploads/2017/08/The-OTA-Shift-FINAL2017.pdf.

Chachra, N., Savage, S., and Voelker, G. M. (2015). Affiliate Crookies: Characterizing Affiliate Marketing Abuse. *IMC '15: Proceedings of the 2015 Internet Measurement Conference*, 41–47. DOI: 10.1145/2815675.2815720.

Cheng, C., Zhong, H., and Cao, L. (2020). Facilitating speed of internationalization: the roles of business intelligence and organizational agility. *Journal of Business Research*, 110, 95–103. DOI: 10.1016/j.jbusres.2020.01.003.

Chuttur, M. Y. (2009). Overview of the Technology Acceptance Model: Origins, Developments and Future Directions. *Sprouts: Working Papers on Information Systems*, 9(37), 1–21. Retrieved 13/03/2020, from https://aisel.aisnet.org/cgi/viewcontent.cgi?article=1289&context=sprouts_all.

Daniele, R., Frew, A. J., Varini, K., and Magakian, A. (2009). Affiliate Marketing in Travel and Tourism. In W. Höpken, U. Gretzel & R. Law (eds.) *Information and Communication Technologies in Tourism 2009* (pp. 343–354). Springer.

Datapine, 2020. *Die 10 besten BI Tools im Jahr 2020 im Vergleich [The 10 best BI tools of the year 2020 by comparison]*. Retrieved 16/04/2020, from https://www.datapine.com/de/artikel/bi-tools-software-loesungen-vergleich.

Deges, F. (2020). *Grundlagen des E-Commerce. Strategien, Modelle, Instrumente [Fundamentals of e-commerce. Strategies, models, instruments].* Springer Gabler. DOI: 10.1007/978-3-658-26320-1.

Denzin, I. (2019). *Playbook Affiliate Marketing.* Retrieved 23/03/2020, from https://www.saphirsolution.de/affiliate-marketing-playbook/.

Denzin, S. (2020). *Der Online Marketing Mix [The online marketing mix].* Retrieved 16/04/2020, from https://www.saphirsolution.de/online-marketing-mix/#gref.

Dremel, C., Herterich, M. M., Wulf, J., and vom Brocke, J. (2020). Actualizing big data analytics affordances: A revelatory case study. *Information & Management*, 57(1), 1–21. DOI: 10.1016/j.im.2018.10.007.

Duffy, D.L. (2004). Multi-channel marketing in the retail environment. *Journal of Consumer Marketing*, 21 (5), pp. 356–359. DOI: 10.1108/07363760410549177.

Duffy, D. L. (2005). Affiliate marketing and its impact on e-commerce. *Journal of Consumer Marketing*, 22 (3), pp. 161–163. DOI: 10.1108/07363760510595986.

Durcevic, S. (2018). *6 Case Studies on The Benefits of Business Intelligence And Analytics.* Retrieved 26/02/2020, from https://www.datapine.com/blog/benefits-of-business-intelligence-and-business-analytics/.

Dwivedi, Y., Rana N., and Alryalat, M. (2017). Affiliate marketing: An overview and analysis of emerging literature. *The Marketing Review*, 17(1), 33–50. DOI: 10.1362/146934717X14909733966092.

Edelman, B. and Brandi, W. (2015). Risk, Information, and Incentives in Online Affiliate Marketing. *Journal of Marketing Research*, 52 (1), 1–12. DOI: 10.1509/jmr.13.0472.

Espinet, J. M. (2019). Big Data in Online Travel Agencies and Its Application Through Electronic Devices. In M. Sigala, R. Rahimi & M. Thelwall (eds.) *Big Data and Innovation in Tourism, Travel and Hospitality. Managerial Approaches, Techniques, and Applications* (pp. 31–55). Springer. DOI: 10.1007/978-981-13-6339-9_3.

Eurowings, 2020. *Das Eurowings Affiliate Programm. Werden Sie Teil des Eurowings Partnerprogramms! [The Eurowings affiliate program. Become a part of the Eurowings partner program!].* Retrieved, 04/03/2020, from https://www.eurowings.com/de/informieren/ueber-uns/unternehmen/affiliate.html.

Frates, J. and Sharp, S. (2005). Using Business Intelligence to Discover New Market Opportunities. *Journal of Competitive Intelligence and Management*,

3(3), 16–28. Retrieved 13/03/2020, from http://www.sharpmarket.com/wp-content/pdfs/article-new-market-opps.pdf.

Gaardboe, R. and Svarre, T. (2018). Business intelligence success factors: a literature review. *Journal of Information Technology Management*, 29(1), 1–5. Retrieved 13/03/2020, from http://jitm.ubalt.edu/XXIX-1/article1.pdf.

Gluchowski, P., Gabriel, R., and Dittmar, C. (2008). *Management Support Systeme und Business Intelligence. Computergestütze Informationssysteme für Fach- und Führungskräfte [Management support systems and business intelligence. Computer-assisted information systems for professionals and executives]* (2nd edition). Springer. DOI: 10.1007/978-3-540-68269-1.

Gregori, N., Daniele, R., and Altinay, L. (2014). Affiliate Marketing in Tourism: Determinants of Consumer Trust. *Journal of Travel Research*, 53 (2), 196–210. DOI: 10.1177/0047287513491333.

Grublješič, T. and Jaklič, J. (2015). Business Intelligence Acceptance: The Prominence of Organizational Factors. *Information Systems Management*, 32(4), 299–315. DOI: 10.1080/10580530.2015.1080000.

Haimson, O. L., Bowser, A. E., Melcer, E. F., and Churchhill, E. F. (2015). Online Inspiration and Exploration for Identity Reinvention. *CHI '15 CHI Conference on Human Factors in Computing Systems*, 3809–3818. DOI: 10.1145/2702123.2702270.

Holland, H. (2019). *Dialogmarketing und Kundenbindung mit Connected Cars. Wie Automobilherstellern mit Daten und Vernetzung die optimale Customer Experience gelingt [Dialogmarketing and customer bonding with connected cars. How automotive manufacturers can succeed an ideal customer experience with the assistance of data and connectivity]*. Springer Gabler. DOI: 10.1007/978-3-658-22929-0.

Hostmann, B. and Hagerty, J. (2010). *ITScore for Business Intelligence and Performance Management*. Retrieved 13/03/2020, from ftp://public.dhe.ibm.com/software/data/sw-library/cognos/pdfs/analystreports/ar_it_score_for_business_intelligence_and_performance_mgmnt.pdf.

Huang, S., McIntosh, S., Sobolevsky, S., and Hung, P. C. K. (2017). Big Data Analytics and Business Intelligence in Industry. *Information Systems Frontiers*, 19 (6), 1229–1232. DOI: 10.1007/s10796-017-9804-9.

iProspect, (2020). *10 Gruende warum Affiliate Marketing in den Online Marketing Mix gehoert [10 reasons why affiliate marketing belongs into the online marketing mix]*. Retrieved 12/04/2020, from https://www.iprospect.com/de/de/news-and-views/news/10-gruende-warum-affiliate-marketing-in-den-online-marketing-mix-gehoert/.

Kärner, S. (2016). *10 Tipps für dein Affiliate-Marketing [10 tips for your affiliate marketing]*. Retrieved 05/04/2020, from https://www.gruenderszene.de/allgemein/affiliate-marketing-tipps?interstitial.

Kasilingam, R. and Thanuja, V. (2020). Recent trends in digital marketing. *UGC Care Journal*, 40(3), 4215–4224. Retrieved 13/04/2020, from https://archives.tpnsindia.org/index.php/sipn/article/view/1058/1006.

Kellermann, M. (2019). *Teil 2: Welche Auswirkungen hat das Planet49-Urteil auf Affiliate-Cookie-Tracking [Part 2: Which consequences has the Planet49-sentence on the affiliate cookie tracking]*. Retrieved 04/03/2020, from https://www.xpose360.de/planet49-affiliate-marketing/.

Kemper, H., Baars, H., and Mehanna, W. (2010). *Business Intelligence – Grundlagen und praktische Anwendungen. Eine Einführung in die IT-basierte Managementunterstützung [Business intelligence – fundamentals and practical applications. An introduction into IT-based management support]* (3rd edition). Vieweg+Teubner. DOI: 10.1007/978-3-8348-9727-5.

Knapke, T. and Olbrich, S. (2016). Capabilities to achieve business intelligence agility – research model and tentative results. *PACIS 2016 Proceedings*. Retrieved 13/03/2020, from https://aisel.aisnet.org/pacis2016/35/.

Koch, T. and Windsperger, J. (2017). Seeing through the network: Competitive advantage in the digital economy. *Journal of Organization Design*, 6 (1), 1–30. DOI: 10.1186/s41469-017-0016-z.

Kollmann, T., Suckow, C., and Peschl, A. (2015). Die Besonderheiten des Gründungsmarketings für Internet-Unternehmen [The features of foundation marketing for internet businesses]. In J. Freiling & T. Kollmann (eds.) *Entrepreneurial Marketing. Besonderheiten, Aufgaben und Lösungsansätze für Gründungsunternehmen [Entrepreneurial marketing. Features, functions and solution approaches for founding companies]* (2nd edition) (pp. 155–174). Springer Gabler. DOI: 10.1007/978-3-658-05026-9.

Kumar, U. D. (2017). *Business Analytics. The Science of Data-Driven Decision Making*. Wiley.

Kundenwachstum.de, (2020). *Banner Marketing – Wie funktioniert das? [Banner advertising – how does that work?]*. Retrieved 10/04/2020, from https://kundenwachstum.de/banner-marketing/.

Lammenett, E. (2007). *TYPO3 Online-Marketing-Guide. Affiliate- und E-Mail-Marketing, Keyword-Advertising, Suchmaschinen-Optimierung mit TYPO3 [TYPO3 online marketing guide. Affiliate- and e-mail marketing, keyword advertising, search engine optimisation with TYPO3]*. Springer Gabler. DOI: 10.1007/978-3-8349-9211-6.

Lammenett, E. (2015). *Praxiswissen Online-Marketing. Affiliate- und E-Mail-Marketing, Suchmaschinenmarketing, Online-Werbung, Social Media, Online-PR [Practical knowledge of online marketing. Affiliate and email marketing, search engine marketing, online advertising, social media, online PR]* (5th edition). Springer Gabler. DOI: 10.1007/978-3-658-09003-6.

Lammenett, E. (2019). *Praxiswissen Online-Marketing. Affiliate-, Influencer-, Content und Email-Marketing, Google Ads, SEO, Social Media, Online-inklusive Facebook-Werbung [Practical knowledge of online marketing. Affiliate-, influencer-, content- and email-marketing, Google Ads, SEO, social media, online- including facebook-marketing]* (7th edition). Springer Gabler. DOI: 10.1007/978-3-658-25135-2.

Larson, D. and Chang, V. (2016). A review and future direction of agile, business intelligence, analytics and data science. *International Journal of Information Management*, 36(5), 700–710. DOI: 10.1016/j.ijinfomgt.2016.04.013.

Lastminute (2020). *Reise-Affiliate: mit Partner-Programm Geld verdienen [Travel-affiliate: Earning money with a partner program]*. Retrieved 30/03/2020, from https://www.lastminute.de/info/affiliate-programm.html.

Lehnen, J. (2017). *Integration von Lead Usern in die Innovationspraxis. Eine empirische Analyse der praktischen Anwendung des Lead User-Ansatzes [Integration of lead users in the practice of innovation. An empirical analysis of the practical application of the lead user approach]*. Springer Gabler. DOI: 10.1007/978-3-658-19385-0_4.

Libai, B., Biyalogorsky, E., and Gerstner, E. (2003). Setting Referral Fees in Affiliate Marketing. *Journal of Service Research*, 5 (4), 303–315. DOI: 10.1177/1094670503251111.

Littmann, U. (2020). *Wann ist welches der 4P des Marketing Mix besonders wichtig? [When is which of the 4Ps from the marketing mix particularly relevant?]*. Retrieved 14/04/2020, from https://www.produktmarketingberatung.de/4p/.

Mariussen, A., Bowie, D., and Paraskevas, A. (2012). *Affiliate marketing optimisation in hospitality and tourism: a multiple stakeholder perspective*. Retrieved 10/04/2020, from https://pdfs.semanticscholar.org/8818/8b3a8d63e1557fa4bbbe659ea22ad6560776.pdf?_ga=2.140253303.557583232.1587388872-495558603.1586873665.

Middleton, V. T. C., Fyall, A., Morgan, M., and Ranchhod, A. (2009). *Marketing in Travel and Tourism* (4th edition). Butterworth-Heinemann.

Mohamed, H. A. E. S. and Fahmy, T. M. (2013). What Factors Influence Consumers' Trust in Travel Affiliate Websites?. *Journal of Faculty of Tourism* *and Hotels*, 7 (2), 120–138. Retrieved 10/04/2020, from https://pdfs.semanticscholar.org/8526/f1664bd604e492cacc382ebf59f9604c1c4e.pdf?_ga=2.127055945.557583232.1587388872-495558603.1586873665.

Mohanta, B, Nanda, P., and Patnaik, S. (2020). Management of V.U.C.A. (Volatility, Uncertainty, Complexity and Ambiguity): Using Machine Learning Techniques in Industry 4.0 Paradigm. In S. Patnaik (ed.) *New Paradigm of Industry 4.0. Internet of Things, Big Data & Cyber Physical Systems* (pp. 1–24). Springer. DOI: 10.1007/978-3-030-25778-1.

Morozan, C. and Enache, E. (2013). Online Performance Through the Affiliate Marketing. *Ovidius University Annals: ECONOMIC SCIENCES SERIES*, 13(1), 880–884. Retrieved 05/04/2020, from http://stec.univ-ovidius.ro/html/anale/ENG/cuprins%20rezumate/volum2013p1.pdf.

Mousavi, S. S. (2012). *Effective Elements on E-Marketing strategy in Tourism Industry*. Retrieved 10/04/2020, from https://ubt.opus.hbz-nrw.de/opus45-ubtr/frontdoor/deliver/index/docId/543/file/Seyed_Siamak_Mousav_Effective_Elements_on_E_Marketing_strategy_in_Tourism_Industry.pdf.

Olbrich, R., Schultz, C. D., and Bormann, P. M. (2019). The effect of social media and advertising activities on affiliate marketing. *International Journal of Internet Marketing and Advertising*, 13 (1), 47–72. DOI: 10.1504/IJIMA.2019.10019165.

Olbrich, R., Schultz, C. D., and Holsing, C. (2019). *Electronic Commerce und Online Marketing. Ein einführendes Lehr- und Übungsbuch [Electronic commerce and online marketing. An introductory text- and practicebook]* (2nd edition). Springer Gabler. DOI: 10.1007/978-3-662-58067-7.

Oliveira, C., Guimarães, T., Portela, F., and Santos, M. (2019). Benchmarking Business Analytics Techniques in Big Data. *Procedia Computer Science*, 160, 690–695. DOI: 10.1016/j.procs.2019.11.026.

Onlinemarketing-Praxis (2020). *Definition Inlineframe (iframe)*. Retrieved 16/04/2020, from https://www.onlinemarketing-praxis.de/glossar/inlineframe-iframe.

Pathak, S. K. and Saxena, R. (2019). Study of Online Marketing: Challenges and Opportunities. *International Journal of Research in Engineering, Science and Management*, 2(8), 350–355. Retrieved 01/04/2020, from https://www.ijresm.com/Vol.2_2019/Vol2_Iss8_August19/IJRESM_V2_I8_95.pdf.

Patrick, Z. and Hee, O. C. (2019). Factors Influencing the Intention to Use Affiliate Marketing: A Conceptual Analysis. *International Journal of Academic Research in Business and Social Sciences*, 9(2), 701–710. DOI: 10.6007/IJARBSS/v9-i2/5608.

Perret, J. K. and Edler, R. (2018). *Who influences the influencer – A Network Analytical Study of Influencer Marketing*. Retrieved 05/04/2020, from https://www.academia.edu/download/56890308/main1802.pdf.

Petersen, D. (2017). Affiliate Marketing. In E. Theobald (ed.) *Brand Evolution. Moderne Markenführung im digitalen Zeitalter [Brand evolution. Modern branding in the digital era]* (2nd edition) (pp. 300–345). Springer Gabler. DOI: 10.1007/978-3-658-15816-3.

Popescu, M., Nicolae, F., and Pavel, M. (2015). Tourism and hospitality industry in the digital era: general overview. *Proceedings of the INTERNATIONAL MANAGEMENT CONFERENCE*, 9(1), 163–168. Retrieved 25/02/2020, from http://conference.management.ase.ro/archives/2015/pdf/17.pdf.

Porter, M. and Millar, V. (1985). How Information Gives You Competitive Advantage. *Harvard Business Review*, 63 (4), 149–160. Retrieved 05/04/2020, from https://profesores.virtual.uniandes.edu.co/~isis1404/dokuwiki/lib/exe/fetch.php?media=bibliografia:10_how_information_gives_you_competitive_advantage.pdf.

Pribisalić, M., Jugo, I., and Martinčić-Ipšić, S. (2019). Selecting a Business Intelligence Solution that is Fit for Business Requirements. *Conference proceedings / 32nd Bled eConference Humanizing Technology for a Sustainable Society*, 443–465. DOI: 10.18690/978-961-286-280-0.24.

Provost, F. and Fawcett, T. (2013). Data science and its relationship to big data and data-driven decision making. *Big Data*, 1 (1), 51–59. DOI: 10.1089/Big.2013.1508.

Prussakov, E. (2011). *Affiliate Program Management: An Hour A Day*. Sybex.

Purnamasari, A. M., Pah, C. E. A., Yoga, M. D. I., Girsang, A. S., and Isa, S. M. (2019). Business Intelligent in an E-Commerce Industry. *IPO Conference Series Materials Science and Engineering*, 598, (pp. 1–8). DOI: 10.1088/1757-899X/598/1/012085.

Pyae, A. (2018). *Cloud Computing in Business Intelligence*. Retrieved 23/02/2020, from https://www.researchgate.net/publication/333037033_Cloud_Computing_in_Business_Intelligence.

Rabhi, L., Falih, N., Afraites, A., and Bouikhalene, B. (2019). Big Data Approach and its Applications in Various Fields: Review. *Procedia Computer Science*, 155, 599–605. DOI: 10.1016/j.procs.2019.08.084.

Rafferty, W., Rafferty, L., and Hung, P. C. K. (2016). Introduction to Big Data. In P. C. K. Hung (ed.) *Big Data Applications and Use Cases* (pp. 1–15). Springer. DOI: 10.1007/978-3-319-30146-4_2.

Rajterič, I. H. (2010). Overview of business intelligence maturity models. *Management*, 15(1), 47–67. Retrieved 23/03/2020, from https://www.researchgate.net/publication/285787090_Overview_of_business_intelligence_maturity_models/stats.

Ram, J., Zhang, C., and Koronios, A. (2016). The implications of Big Data analytics on Business Intelligence: A qualitative study in China. *Procedia Computer Science*, 87, 221–226. DOI: 10.1016/j.procs.2016.05.152.

Rhyn, M. and Blohm, I. (2019). Patterns of Data-Driven Decision-Making: How Decision-Makers Leverage Crowdsourced Data. *ICIS 2019 Proceedings*, 1–17. Retrieved 16/04/2020, from https://aisel.aisnet.org/icis2019/crowds_social/crowds_social/31/.

Scherer, R., Siddiq, F., and Tondeur, J. (2019). The technology acceptance model (TAM): A meta-analytic structural equation modelling approach to explaining teachers' adoption of digital technology in education. *Computers & Education*, 128, 13–35. DOI: 10.1016/j.compedu.2018.09.009.

Schilling, B. (2019). *Grundlagen des Marketing: Einführung, Konzeption, Print, Online, Werbung, Branding, Media, PR, Marketingmix [Fundamentals of marketing: Introduction, conception, print, online, advertising, branding, media, PR, marketing mix]* (3rd edition). Books on Demand.

Schön, D. (2016). *Planung und Reporting. Grundlagen, Business Intelligence, Mobile BI und Big-Data-Analytics. [Planning and reporting. Fundamentals, business intelligence, mobile BI and big data analytics]* (2nd edition). Springer Gabler. DOI: 10.1007/978-3-658-08009-9.

Septiawan, P., Nadra, N. M., and Astuti, N. N. S. (2018). Contribution of offline and online travel agent toward room occupancy at four points by Sheraton Bali Seminyak Hotel. *Journal of Applied Sciences in Travel and Hospitality*, 1(1), 24–33. Retrieved 10/04/2020, from http://ojs.pnb.ac.id/index.php/JASTH/article/view/909.

Shaaban, E., Helmy, Y., Khedr, A., and Nasr, M. (2012). Business Intelligence Maturity Models: Toward New Integrated Model. *The 12th International Arab Conference on Information Technology (ACIT)*, 276–284. Retrieved, 22/03/2020, from https://core.ac.uk/download/pdf/80743005.pdf.

Shirisha, M. (2018). Digital Marketing Importance in the New Era. *International Journal of Engineering Technology Science and Research*, 5 (1), 612–617. Retrieved 10/04/2020, from http://www.ijetsr.com/images/short_pdf/1516243010_612-617-SJ51_ISSN10.pdf.

Skyrius, R., Katin, I., Kazimianec, M., Nemitko, S., Rumšas, G., and Žilinskas, R. (2016). Factors Driving Business Intelligence Culture. *Issues in Informing Science and Information Technology*, 13, 171–178. DOI: 10.28945/3420.

Unternehmer.de (2020). *Pay per Lead.* Retrieved 03/03/2020, from https://unternehmer.de/lexikon/online-marketing-lexikon/pay-per-lead.

Smith, A. (2020). *Consumer Behaviour and Analytics.* Routledge.

Srinivas, P., Priya, K., and Pinky, M. (2018). Travel from traditional marketing to digital marketing. *Shanlax International Journal of Commerce*, 6 (2), 229–241. Retrieved 12/03/2020, from http://www.primaxijcmr.com/wp-content/uploads/2018/06/Full-Book.pdf#page=243.

Suchada, J., Watanapa, B., Charoenkitkarn, N., and Chirapornchai, T. (2017). Hotels and resorts rent intention via online affiliate marketing. *IAIT Conference Proceedings*, 132–142. DOI: 10.18502/kss.v3i1.1402.

Tableau (2020). *What is business intelligence? Your guide to BI and why it matters.* Retrieved 05/04/2020, from https://www.tableau.com/learn/articles/business-intelligence.

Troyanos, K. (2020). *Use data to answer your key business questions.* Retrieved 06/04/2020, from https://hbr.org/2020/02/use-data-to-answer-your-key-business-questions.

Vila, T. D. and González, E. A. (2020). CRM as a key element in online commercialization: Analysis of tourism search and metasearch engines. In A. Rocha, A. Abreu, J. V. de Carvalho, D. Liberato, E. A. González & P. Lieberato (eds.) *Advances in Tourism, Technology and Smart Systems. Proceedings of ICOTTS 2019* (pp. 173–188). Springer. DOI: 10.1007/978-981-15-2024-2.

Wandiger, P. (2020). *Welche Provisionsmodelle gibt es im Affiliate Marketing und was ist das beste? [Which commission models exist in affiliate marketing and which one is the best?].* Retrieved 06/04/2020, from https://www.affiliate-marketing-tipps.de/affiliate-marketing/welche-provisionsmodelle-gibt-es-im-affiliate-marketing/100134/.

Wauyo, F., Omol, E., and Okumu, J. (2017). Effectiveness of business intelligence technology absorptive capacity and innovation competency of university staff, case of Uganda University Mbale Campus. *European Journal of Technology*, 1 (2), 55–73. Retrieved 13/03/2020, from https://ajpojournals.org/journals/index.php/EJT/article/view/223/329.

Williams, S (2016). *Business Intelligence Strategy and Big Data Analytics. A General Management Perspective.* Morgan Kaufmann.

Willmert, M. and Nayak, M. (2019). Role of OTAs and MSEs in individual hotels' distribution policy in the Central Moselle. In C. Maurer & H. J. Siller (eds.) *ISCONTOUR 2019 Tourism Research Perspectives. Proceedings of the International Student Conference in Tourism Research* (pp. 314–327). Books on Demand.

Yu, E., Lapouchnian, A., and Deng, S. (2013). Adapting to Uncertain and Evolving Enterprise Requirements. *IEEE 7th International Conference on Research Challenges in Information Science (RCIS)*, 1–12. DOI:10.1109/RCIS.2013.6577687.

Zhou, Z., Chawla, N. V., Jin, Y., and Williams, G. J. (2014). Big Data Opportunities and Challenges: Discussions from Data Analytics Perspectives. *IEEE Computational Intelligence Magazine*, 9 (4), 62–74. DOI. 10.1109/MCI.2014.2350953.

Zimmermann, T. (2011). Digitale Markenführung mit Affiliate Marketing [Digital branding with affiliate marketing]. In E. Theobald & P. T. Haisch (eds.) *Brand Evolution. Moderne Markenführung im digitalen Zeitalter [Brand evolution. Modern branding in the digital era]* (1st edition) (pp. 291–310). Springer Gabler. DOI: 10.1007/978-3-8349-6913-2_17.

Appendix I – Interview Guidelines

Part 1 (Business Intelligence & Affiliate Marketing)

D: Vielen Dank, dass Sie sich für das Interview zur Verfügung stellen. Bitte stellen Sie sich kurz einmal vor und geben Sie Ihren beruflichen Werdegang in den Bereichen Affiliate- und Reise-Marketing wieder.

E: Thank you for participating in the interview. Please introduce yourself and give an overview about your work experience in the fields of affiliate and travel marketing.

D: Für wie wichtig schätzen Sie Business Intelligence im Bereich des Targetings von Affiliate Kampagnen ein? Bietet es Unternehmen neue Möglichkeiten, die es vorher und evtl. sogar auch im Offline Marketing nicht gab (wenn ja, welche)? Bitte gehen Sie auf Targeting und Retargeting ein.

E: How would you bring business intelligence into line with the targeting of affiliate campaigns? Does it offer corporations more targeting opportunities than before or in the offline marketing (if yes, which ones)? Please refer to targeting and retargeting.

D: Wie schätzen Sie den Einfluss von Business Intelligence auf Marketingentscheidungen im Affiliate Bereich ein? Wird es Ihrer Meinung nach ausreichend genutzt oder besteht hier noch Verbesserungspotenzial?

E: How would you value the influence of business intelligence on affiliate marketing decisions? Do you think that it is used sufficiently or is there more potential to that?

D: Welche gesammelten Daten sind Ihrer Ansicht nach am wertvollsten für das Affiliate-Marketing und die damit verbundenen Entscheidungen?

E: Which data collected do you assess as the most relevant for affiliate marketing and the respective decisions involved?

D: Würden Sie sagen, dass der Einsatz von Business Intelligence die durchgeführten Affiliate-Marketing Kampagnen effizienter gestaltet? Wenn ja, inwiefern?

E: Would you say that the usage of business intelligence increases the efficiency of affiliate marketing campaigns? If yes, how?

D: Gibt es Business Intelligence Best Practices oder Must-Dos, die Sie für das Affiliate-Marketing empfehlen würden?

E: Are there any business intelligence best practices or must-dos that you would recommend for affiliate marketing?

D: Gibt es Grenzen in der Nutzung von Business Intelligence im Affiliate Bereich? Wenn ja, welche?

E: Are there limitations in using business intelligence for affiliate marketing purposes? If yes, which ones?

D: Wie schätzen Sie die Weiterentwicklung von der Beziehung zwischen Business Intelligence und Affiliate-Marketing ein?

E: How do you assess the development of the relationship between business intelligence and affiliate marketing?

PART 2 (AFFILIATE MARKETING & TRAVEL MARKETING)

D: Wie schätzen Sie den Erfolg von Affiliate-Marketing im Reise-Marketing ein? Bitte gehen Sie auf die Bereiche Brand Awareness, Neukundengewinnung und Reaktivierung bestehender Kunden ein.

E: How would you asses the success of affiliate marketing in the field of travel marketing?
Please refer to the fields of brand awareness, customer acquisition and reactivation of existing customers.

D: Sehen Sie im Affiliate-Marketing, als Reise-Marketing Kanal, einen Vorteil/mehrere Vorteile gegenüber anderen Online-Marketing Kanälen? Wenn ja, welchen/welche?

E: Do you think that affiliate marketing, as a travel marketing channel, has an advantage(s) towards other online marketing channels? If yes, which?

D: Gibt es Ihrer Meinung nach auch irgendwelche Nachteile?

E: Do you think that there might be disadvantages, too?

D: Inwiefern hilft Business Intelligence gezielt die richtigen Kunden im Reise-Marketing per Affiliate-Marketing anzusprechen?

E: To what extend does business intelligence help travel companies to target the right clients via affiliate marketing?

D: Gibt Business Intelligence Ihrer Erfahrung nach Firmen der Reisebranche einen Wettbewerbsvorteil in Bezug auf die durchgeführten Affiliate-Marketing Tätigkeiten?

E: Based on your experience, does business intelligence give businesses of the travel industry a competitive advantage referred to affiliate marketing actions?

Internet Economics / Internetökonomie
edited by / hrsg. von Prof. Dr. Julia Maintz (Cologne Business School (CBS))

Athanasios Andreou
Interaktives Zusammenwirken zwischen Unternehmen, Nutzern und Online Communities: Zur Optimierung von Innovationsprozessen
Innovationen sind die Voraussetzung für den langfristigen Erfolg von Unternehmen. Jedoch erreicht eine überwältigende Mehrheit innovativer Lösungen nie die Marktreife. Als ein Hauptgrund dafür wird die fehlende Orientierung an Marktbedürfnissen angesehen. In diesem Buch werden daher Möglichkeiten aufgezeigt, wie durch die interaktive Zusammenarbeit zwischen Unternehmen, visionären Nutzern und Entwicklern von Produkten sowie Online Communities Innovationsprozesse dahingehend optimiert werden können, dass erfolgreiche Innovationen entwickelt werden.
Bd. 10, 2016, 86 S., 24,90 €, br., ISBN 978-3-643-13197-3

LIT Verlag Berlin – Münster – Wien – Zürich – London
Auslieferung Deutschland / Österreich / Schweiz: siehe Impressumsseite

Mohammad-Munir Adi

The Usage of Social Media in the Arab Spring

The Potential of Media
to Change Political Landscapes
throughout the Middle East and Africa

Internet Economics / Internetökonomie Bd. 8

LIT

Mohammad-Munir Adi
The Usage of Social Media in the Arab Spring
The Potential of Media to Change Political Landscapes throughout the Middle East and Africa
The unrests, riots, revolutions and civil wars throughout the Arab Spring have undoubtedly initiated a series of chain reactions on Arab and African soil. The research analyzes the usage of the Internet and the Social Media platforms in Tunisia, Egypt and Syria in order to clarify its relevance to the uprisings.
Bd. 8, 2014, 72 S., 19,90 €, br., ISBN 978-3-643-90468-3

LIT Verlag Berlin – Münster – Wien – Zürich – London
Auslieferung Deutschland / Österreich / Schweiz: siehe Impressumsseite

Laura Neises
Social CRM in the airline industry: Engaging the digital natives
Social media has found its way into most businesses as a tool to push sales. Yet its potential to create long-term customer loyalty is not fully exploited. Especially in industries characterized by fierce competition customer loyalty is key for sustainable success. But how can companies attract the future consumers? Born in the digital age, digital natives are powerful experts of social media and will dominate businesses. Building on insights from the aviation industry, this book develops an approach to use social media in a way that engages the digital natives in long-term relationships.
Bd. 7, 2013, 112 S., 17,90 €, br., ISBN 978-3-643-90397-6

Elena Trost
Social Media Marketing in BRIC Countries
Examining case studies of BMW, adidas and NIVEA
The economic growth and increasing Internet access within BRIC (Brazil, Russia, India and China) is opening new opportunities for companies to reach wider audiences.
This study examines these opportunities and assesses how global companies are capitalizing on these emerging markets; in particular the degree to which digital marketing and social CRM through social networks are being used. For the purposes of this analysis, three German brands are examined in detail: BMW, adidas and NIVEA.
The author shows that regular interaction with Internet users and monitoring of social networks can result in companies experiencing an uplift in both public perception and engagement. Another aspect addressed is the cultural variance that needs to be taken into account when planning social media activities. This study concludes that presently the full potential of social media has yet to be utilized within the BRIC countries, and that there is a unique opportunity to be realised by companies.
Bd. 6, 2013, 144 S., 19,90 €, br., ISBN 978-3-643-90264-1

Jana Louise Baum
Mobbing 2.0
Eine kultursoziologische Betrachtung des Phänomens Cyber-Mobbing
Digitale soziale Medien verändern Kommunikationsprozesse. Das Internet als neuer Raum vielfältiger Möglichkeiten bietet eine neue Freiheit, dessen größte Stärken zugleich die größten Risiken bergen. Cyber-Mobbing, ein vielschichtiges Phänomen, das viele, vor allem junge Menschen betrifft, entwickelt sich zu einem auffallend präsenten Thema unserer Gesellschaft. Der vorliegende Band analysiert nicht nur Ergebnisse soziologischer Untersuchungen zu Cyber-Mobbing, sondern liefert zudem eine Betrachtung des Themas aus medien- und kulturwissenschaftlicher Perspektive.
Bd. 5, 2015, 108 S., 19,90 €, br., ISBN 978-3-643-11809-7

LIT Verlag Berlin – Münster – Wien – Zürich – London
Auslieferung Deutschland / Österreich / Schweiz: siehe Impressumsseite